"Doug Wilson tells a fascinating story in *The World Was Our Stage*, a unique personal journey that also recalls the riveting history of the coming-of-age of sports television. Doug is one of the finest and kindest gentlemen to ever work in the business, and it's a delight to go back in time with him as he spans the globe once more to tell the stories that he and his colleagues first told so magnificently decades ago. In Doug's storytelling, it truly still is a wide, and wonderful, world of sports."

Christine Brennan
USA Today national sports columnist, ABC News
commentator, best-selling author of *Inside Edge*

"Doug Wilson revisits a time when *ABC's Wide World of Sports* was must-see TV every weekend for millions of Americans. If some of these stories seem made up—trust me—they're not. I was there for many of them and would walk away thinking, 'You can't make this stuff up.'" It was great fun to witness and just as much fun to read about."

Al Michaels
Emmy Award-winning NBC sportscaster,
previously with ABC Sports for three decades

"Along with my father, Jim McKay, Doug Wilson was in many ways the heart and soul of ABC Sports. Doug's passion for his craft and his remarkable creativity are surpassed only by his storytelling ability, both on television and in print. *The World Was Our Stage* is a fascinating and compassionate behind-the-scenes look at many of the greatest sports television stories and personalities of all time. My father would have loved this book, almost as much as he loved working with Doug."

Sean McManus
Chairman, CBS Sports

"ABC Sports and *Wide World of Sports* not only changed but also virtually created the sports television landscape in the United States and set the standard by which sports coverage around the world is now measured. They had the vision to put the King/Riggs Battle of the Sexes match in prime time and it paid off for them and for Bobby and me, and it raised the profile of tennis worldwide—all while putting social change in the national spotlight. ABC Sports was a game changer and they fully understood the importance of bringing sports to the people."

Billie Jean King
Sports icon and humanitarian;
Cofounder, World Team Tennis

"As Olympic athletes, we always cherished *ABC's Wide World of Sports* for exposing sports like gymnastics to a much wider audience than our sport ever enjoyed before. Doug Wilson, who has been a friend for over thirty years, has always delighted us with his behind-the-scenes stories about this groundbreaking sports television show. We are thrilled that Doug has finally decided to share these incredible stories from the award-winning show that represented a paradigm shift in sports television."

Nadia Comaneci and Bart Conner
Olympic and World champions in gymnastics

"Doug Wilson's sensitivity and his passion for 'getting it right' from the perspective of the athlete continue to define his amazing contributions to television. I love this book, and I couldn't put it down."

Scott Hamilton
1984 Olympic gold medalist in men's figure skating,
four-time World champion

"Everything America knows or loves about figure skating comes from the eyes and heart of Doug Wilson. It was a privilege to work with him."

Lesley Visser
Hall of Fame sportscaster

"Doug Wilson has an elephantine memory. Our decades of working together at ABC Sports took us from Innsbruck, Austria, to Nagano, Japan, to Podunk, USA. I enjoyed reading about the history we shared."

Dick Button
Emmy Award-winning sports analyst,
Olympic and World champion in figure skating

"In addition to all of the interesting and entertaining stories Doug Wilson tells with firsthand knowledge of the people and events that shaped ABC Sports, there is a great deal of history in this book. Not only is there plenty of sports history but also the history of the sports television industry from an insider point of view.

The World Was Our Stage should be required reading for every student of broadcasting. What is documented in this book is critical for understanding the origins of this industry."

Jim Jennett
Emmy Award-winning sports television director

"For fifty years, Doug Wilson embodied the spirit and creative excellence that was ABC Sports. His passionate storytelling played an integral part in the success of *Wide World of Sports*, the longest and most celebrated sports anthology show in television history. Doug allowed the places, events, and athletes to always be in the story. This book relives the lost age of innocence in sports and chronicles its greatest athletes, 'up close and personal.' I was fortunate to produce many of the world's greatest sporting events with Doug, and for that I am grateful."

Curt Gowdy Jr.
Emmy Award-winning executive producer

THE WORLD WAS OUR STAGE

Spanning the Globe with ABC Sports

by **Doug Wilson** with Jody Cohan

Foreword by Peggy Fleming

ISBN: 1490403663
ISBN 13: 9781490403663
Library of Congress Control Number: 2013910770
CreateSpace Independent Publishing Platform
North Charleston, South Carolina

To Debbie, my devoted late wife, who lovingly raised

our three sons while I was routinely in absentia;

and

To those sons, Ted, Jamie, and Peter,

who persevered and continue to make me proud;

and

To Betsy, who showed me that two equals one,

made my life whole again, and filled it with joy.

Contents

Foreword by Peggy Fleming   **xiii**

Scene Set   **1**

Most Valuable Players   **10**

    Roone Pinckney Arledge Jr. 11

    Jim McKay 15

The Greatest   **20**

    Ali 21

    Evel 26

    Nadia 33

Leading Ladies   **42**

    Peggy 45

    Trixi and Janet 50

    Dorothy 55

    E. Z. 59

    Roz 61

    Kat 62

Score! 65

Foggy Day 67

Symphony No. 9 68

East Meets West 70

Sound Bites 72

Craps 72

Cosell 74

Woody 74

King of the Hill 75

Stud Farm 76

High Speed 76

Raquel 77

Grammar Lesson 79

Secretariat 79

Well Preserved 80

Torvill & Dean 81

Whitaker 82

SI Jinx 83

Gold Medal 83

Vignettes from the Voyage 103

  The Boxer 103

  Mrs. Shriver 104

  Humble Howard 106

  Canvas of Ice..107

The Cresta 110

Playing Politics 117

  Technical Foul 118

  Irina 119

  Arthur 123

  Bad Judgment.. 126

  Broad Casting.. 129

Still Rings 137

Closing Ceremony 151

Epilogue 159

Credit Roll 165

Index 173

Foreword by Peggy Fleming

For an athlete whose powerful spirit and eventual legacy are defined by devotion to the advancement of sport, there truly is no greater thrill than victory and no greater agony than defeat. Likewise, for loyal fans and enthusiastic spectators, there is nothing more captivating than experiencing the highs and lows—the emotional triumph and disappointment—alongside the legends and rising stars participating in what was appropriately coined over fifty years ago, "the human drama of athletic competition."

With the launch of *ABC's Wide World of Sports* in 1961, there came a revolution to athletic coverage that propelled us straight into the golden era of sports television. For the first time, ABC literally "spanned the globe" to find new, unusual, or never-before-seen competition and displays of athleticism. This was *the* time when televised sports grew from peripheral interest to daily discussion. During this revolution, the spotlight shifted from merely watching a competition, match, or race to becoming engaged with and emotionally tied to the athlete and his or her journey to greatness.

With this new, intensely intimate, sophisticated, and emotional approach to sports storytelling came a surge of cinematic genius and technical effort, all developed by those pioneers who foresaw the future and devoted themselves to creating it. Roone Arledge and other visionaries set their sights on the big picture—a global community waiting, eager, and willing not only to watch a variety of sports but also to *be* part of the evolving sports landscape. Their dreams were carried out by an elite and talented crew of producers, directors, camera operators, and commentators, including one of ABC Sports' most passionate, devoted, and legendary producer/directors, my friend and colleague, Doug Wilson. Doug spent his exceptionally successful career behind the cameras, tirelessly orchestrating, creating, coordinating, and capturing our generation's greatest sports moments.

Doug was always ahead of his time, exceeding industry expectations at every opportunity. In an era before GoPro video cameras and smartphones, he brought the audience onto the ice or into the ring or over the daredevil's pit in ways never seen before. He pushed the boundaries and worked the angles to capture *the moment* or grab *that look* we'd all remember for decades.

During our years together at ABC Sports, it was not unusual to find Doug (day or night) balancing the rigging, duct taping, and crafting inventive ways to deliver the audience the same dose of adrenaline, wave of emotion, jolt of elation, or sigh of disappointment that the athlete was experiencing during his or her moment of competition. He took great care to capture facial expressions, long lines, and body language, and his regard for the integrity of both athlete and performance shone on the small screen.

Few people have ever conceived of covering the world of sports as Doug did through his eyes and ears. He did things differently from his directing contemporaries. He didn't just video an event. He lived in the moment with the athlete, the camera crew, the audio team, and the entire production unit. He captured the fine details and the grand energies. In this book, *The World Was Our Stage*, he shares his memories with the same approach—showing his love for athlete and sport, setting, and journey—as he did for so many years through the camera lens.

I know that Doug has wanted to share his unique, inspiring, and very personal behind-the-scenes stories for many years now. When you open this book, you will enjoy a trip down memory lane and learn some unknown details about sports' greatest moments. As a skater, I have benefited from Doug's beautiful and artistic storytelling, and I will forever appreciate the attention and thoughtfulness he gave to televising my performances. As a friend, I know how hard he worked in an often unglamorous space, at all hours and with incredible passion, to capture and share a variety of performances. As part of the global audience, I have enjoyed watching the thrill of victory and the agony of defeat as told by someone who truly understands, from all angles, **the human drama of athletic competition.**

1

Scene Set

They crouch in starting blocks, balance on the edge of a three-story platform, pause at center ice, or stare nose-to-nose in the middle of a ring. In the back of a mobile van, we don headsets, lock eyes on monitors, hover over switchers, and direct our cameras. In a sense, we are no different than the athletes we are about to cover. We share the same emotions: butterflies, anticipation, tension, adrenaline—all of it—as the countdown continues: 5…4…3…2…1…

BAM!

Twenty million people are watching what you're doing.

I was addicted to that rush for fifty years as a member of the crew at ABC Sports, the innovator in sports television, and its marquee sports anthology program, *ABC's Wide World of Sports*. During the early years of *Wide World*, many of us on the crew felt we had a calling. Everywhere we went was new, and everything we did was new. Among our television debuts were gymnastics, tennis from Wimbledon, the Indianapolis 500, and surfing.

The effect the show had on its viewers became clear to me when I was about twelve years into my tenure with ABC. My contract was up for renewal, and I was unhappy with the network's offer. I complained about it to a friend over drinks at a bar while on location in Los Angeles. "Do you realize what you do?" she said as she swiveled toward me, her head shaking in consternation. "I was raised in a small town on the eastern slopes of the Rockies. All we had in town was a factory and a dog track. And every Saturday afternoon my friends and I would call each other and decide whose house we were meeting at to eat burgers and watch *Wide World of Sports*. I learned more about geography, politics, and what makes people tick watching the show you work on than I ever did in school!"

To understand the significance and impact of *Wide World of Sports* is to understand the times. The show debuted in 1961, and the times were definitely "a-changin'." In April that year, President John F. Kennedy authorized the Bay of Pigs invasion of Cuba, hoping to ignite an uprising against Fidel Castro. In June, Soviet Premier Nikita Khrushchev reissued an ultimatum to his country's World War II allies to withdraw their armed forces from West Berlin. When the United States, France, and the United Kingdom refused to comply, the Soviets began to build the Berlin Wall. By the end of the year, the United States was involved in combat operations in Vietnam, and Freedom Riders from northern states boarded buses to ride into the South and bravely test the new federal antisegregation laws.

American culture was shifting as well. The fun beat and gyrations of rock 'n' roll gave way to songs of protest, spearheaded by Bob Dylan, and fashion would break out of its staid 1950s' styles with miniskirts, bikinis, and clothing that exploded in psychedelic color. Changes were also afoot in television, which was now in 88 percent of American households. In those decades before cable and the Internet would provide boundless viewing options, the broadcast spectrum limited the number of TV channels. Most big cities had only about seven channels total, and there were just three national networks: the Columbia Broadcasting System (CBS), the National Broadcasting Company (NBC), and the American Broadcasting Company (ABC). ABC was the last to go on the air and struggled to keep up. The network brass knew they had to try something different in order to compete. CEO Leonard Goldenson also had the instinct that merely putting radio on television would not prevail in the long run. He recognized in the 1950s that television was a visual medium that warranted visual programming with action. He tried to tap into the Hollywood motion picture business to produce television shows, but none of the studios were interested. Serendipitously, after Walt and Roy Disney were turned down by the banks—and CBS and NBC—to help finance a new entertainment concept in Southern California called Disneyland, the brothers telephoned Goldenson. ABC-Paramount Television acquired not only a sizeable chunk of Disney, but also a commitment from Disney for a weekly series. As time went on, Goldenson then decided to invest in what had been an undeveloped area of programming by all the networks: sports.

At the time, sports fans had some boxing and only a few professional baseball, football, and basketball games to watch on the weekends. These games were broadcast mostly regionally due to contractual obligations and finite air space. ABC's first move was to contract Sports Programs, Inc., an independent company started by Edgar J. Scherick in 1957. Scherick had acquired the television rights for NCAA football for the 1960 season, giving birth to the now incredibly lucrative business of televising college football. In 1961, ABC bought Sports Programs, Inc., which eventually became ABC Sports, Inc.

To fill the void at the end of the football season, Scherick created a program completely devoted to sports and put a young producer named Roone Arledge at the helm. CBS had its *Sports Spectacular,* also a sports anthology, but *ABC'S Wide World of Sports* would be different. It would travel far and wide and cover sports unfamiliar to the American public. Goldenson doubted the concept and thought it would never be profitable. Nonetheless, he gave his approval. *Wide World of Sports* premiered on April 29, 1961, and featured the Penn Relays from Philadelphia and the Drake Relays from Des Moines. These track meets had never been televised before, and the cutting back and forth between the two events was also a television first. Still, the show got little attention until July, when it covered the USA/USSR track and field meet in Moscow. With the Cold War in full swing and tension high between the two superpowers, all eyes were on Moscow—and ABC—as the US and Soviet teams marched side by side into Lenin Stadium on July 15.

While blacks and whites struggled with civil rights at home and the leaders of the Free World and the Eastern Bloc aimed nuclear missiles at one another, seventy thousand Soviet spectators and millions of American TV viewers watched six world records fall and cheered on a black female sprinter named Wilma Rudolph and a Siberian high jumper named Valery Brumel. The telecast put *Wide World of Sports*, initially intended as a "summer replacement," on the television map.

My first sports assignment came in early 1963, when Roone Arledge needed a fourth associate director for *Wide World of Sports'* telecast of the New York Athletic Club Indoor Games from Madison Square Garden (MSG). I was excited and eager, as I had already become a fan of the show and its host, Jim McKay. Having grown up just twenty miles outside Manhattan in Garden City, New York, I thought of MSG as "sports Mecca," the place where, as a kid, I saw the Knicks play. And there I was in the broadcast booth, handing note cards with the cues for promos and commercial leads to Curt Gowdy, the famous voice of the Boston Red Sox-turned-television sportscaster while Jim Beaty broke the indoor four-minute-mile barrier for only the second time in history!

I didn't grow up dreaming about a career in sports television. Aside from the fact that television didn't even exist when I was a kid, I had other aspirations in mind. Sure, I loved sports—I can still remember watching Jackie Robinson steal home in a game against the Cubs at Ebbets Field in Brooklyn, and I fondly recall sitting on the edge of the tub in the bathroom while my big brother David sat on the can and spun stories from the sports pages. But the truth was, I wanted to be a singer. One of my idols was Perry Como. He hosted a musical variety show on CBS at the time, and I never missed it. He was also a member of the Garden City Country Club, and my parents' house just happened to back up to the fairway of what was then the ninth hole.

See, I had a plan. Perry Como was going to make me a star.

In the summer of 1951, I was fifteen and old enough to start working as a caddy at the club. This meant I was privy to the schedule. When I knew Mr. Como would be on the course, I made my way home. Once, when I saw him walking the ninth fairway, I ran inside and up to the shower, soaped myself up, and with the windows wide open, broke into "Where or When" as loud as I could. I hoped and prayed that the dulcet tones of my second tenor voice would waft across the yard, through the birch and cherry trees, and across the colonial bent grass right as Mr. Como was taking his backswing. Utterly impressed, I figured, he would drop his nine iron, follow the sound of my voice through the break in the hedges, head up the porch steps into the house...and make me a star.

My plan didn't work.

I would have to wait another two years for the perfect opportunity to approach Mr. Como. During a semifinal match for the club championship, I waited for him on the eighteenth green. In my mind, I tried to put together words that would be appropriate—words that would somehow make him like me. As my confidence began to wane, I reminded myself that I was a well-rounded, all-American boy. I was president of my senior class and an Eagle Scout. I had lettered in soccer, wrestling, track, and tennis, had won two intramural boxing championships, and would soon be on my way to Colgate University on a scholarship. Everything was possible. The future looked great.

Nevertheless, I was about to run off in a panic. Then Mr. Bachial, a friend of my parents, spotted me and asked what I was doing there. After I blurted out that I wanted to meet Mr. Como, Mr. B. said he would introduce me. A few minutes later, right there on the apron of the green, I was talking to Perry Como! Unfortunately, I didn't know what to say beyond the usual pleasantries.

"Well, what do you want?" Mr. Como gently asked.

My mind fluttered, and out of nowhere came words I felt comfortable saying: "I would like to come watch your rehearsal." Mr. Como then told me to be at the stage door on Fifty-Third Street between Broadway and Eighth Avenue at 1:00 p.m. the following day.

I could hardly contain my excitement as I left Garden City in my parents' 1949 Dodge and headed for the Big Apple. Despite having been pulled over on the Queensboro Bridge for running a red light, I arrived on time. Mr. Como personally greeted me at the stage door and even walked me to my seat. Like most programming in the evolving medium of television, *The Chesterfield Supper Club* (named for its cigarette-company sponsor), was broadcast live, so the atmosphere was frenetic. As singers rehearsed on the stage that was dressed to look like a pier, the lighting director painted the scene with colored lights—a shocking contrast to the shades of gray that appeared on my TV at home. The orchestra rehearsed, cue card guys scrambled about, and the director boomed in now and then over the PA system about positioning. Then everything got still. The lights dimmed, strains of slide guitar filled the air, and there appeared Perry Como, seated on a bench upstage.

"I saw the harbor lights," he began to croon. "They only told me we were parting…" He rose from the bench as he continued singing and took only a few steps downstage toward the camera. My eyes then shifted to the fuzzy black and white moving image on the audience TV monitor. It looked as if he had walked thirty feet! And it all looked so real on that tiny twelve-inch screen! I was fascinated by the illusion.

The entire experience left me moonstruck for sure, but I was completely unaware that I had just glimpsed my future.

There were no openings for "star" when I graduated from Colgate in 1957, so I had to pursue other options. Through an alumni connection, I landed an NBC page position—despite having flipped over a footstool at the conclusion of my interview. I would be earning $49.50 a week, just enough to cover my train rides back and forth to Manhattan from my parents' house.

My draft notice arrived in January of 1958. I served six months of active duty in the United States Air Force Reserves, right between the end of the Korean War and the beginning of the Vietnam War. That September, I married Debbie Grigg, whom I'd met at a gathering of college a cappella singing groups. As a husband, I needed to make more money. No production jobs were available at NBC, so through another Colgate alumnus, I interviewed for a production assistant opening over at ABC. I got the job. The day after that, I was holding cue cards for singer Pat Boone and bringing home $60 a week—and hoping I would be in his white buckskin shoes one day.

I was later assigned to *The Dick Clark Show*. With Mr. Clark's help, I recorded a single for Roulette Records called "Have Love Will Travel" and lip-synched it on *American Bandstand*. Regrettably, no one stepped forward to offer me my own TV music hour. Just when I thought I would have to get into another line of work to support my family, I learned that I had been promoted to associate director—at the very livable wage of $158.50 a week.

When I got the offer to work for the sports department full time in 1963, Debbie and I sat down to talk about it. I had little experience in location work, and such credits would be great to add to my résumé. The one glaring drawback? The extensive travel. Two of our three children had already been born, but we decided that we could manage the demands that would be facing both of us for the next few years.

Have love, will travel! Those two years turned into fifty. The stars aligned for *Wide World of Sports* as the jet age ushered in aircraft powered by turbine engines instead of propellers. Faraway destinations became reachable within hours instead of days, and recently launched satellites enabled global communications, even if they weren't so instant in those days. Every kid in America who tuned into *Wide World* could now picture himself or herself racing through the streets of Monte Carlo, diving off a coastal cliff in Acapulco, or hurtling headfirst down a treacherous ice track in St. Moritz. We were the first to air a live sporting event via satellite in 1965 with the 24 Hours of Le Mans race in France, and we were breaking other technical ground as well. We rigged cameras to the top of mobile units to capture the speed and movement of sport; we edited footage—thanks to the invention of videotape—to create pacing and heighten tension; and we tried new perspectives with gimmicks such as underwater cameras, which could have electrified the swimming pool!

But it wasn't just all our "firsts" and the new technology that made *Wide World* so appealing. It was our *approach* to sports. To us, sports were more than the playing, winning, and losing of athletic contests. Sporting events were dramas. Live theater. And the only difference between a performance on a stage and a clash on the field is that on stage, the script has already been written. Before going on the air to cover an event, we would discuss potential plot lines and how we might follow them—but the truth was that we had no control over what was going to happen. As Jim McKay used to say, "We make a plan from which to change."

So we set the scene for our viewers by introducing the host city and its environs, history, and customs, whether it was Natchitoches,

Louisiana, or Beijing, China. Then we would introduce the court, the field, or key apparatus—anything from a gauntlet glove to a pommel horse. Most importantly, we gave our "characters," the athletes, relevance with our "Up Close and Personal" profiles to help viewers relate to—and care—about them. And finally, during the competition or game itself, we would have expert commentators—the first network to do so—telling you what the g-forces feel like while doing three-and-a-half somersaults off a ten-meter platform or what goes through a stockcar driver's mind while driving door handle to door handle at two-hundred miles per hour in a pack of thirty cars.

On occasion, our broadcasts had impact beyond the sporting world, as they did in 1972, when we headed to Munich and the Games of the XX Olympiad. We arrived to find the Bavarian capital draped in peaceful pastel colors to hide the cloud of Nazism that the German hosts hoped to blow away with the winds of time. Tragically, eleven days into the Games, an Arab terrorist group took eleven Israeli team members hostage in the Olympic Village. The Games were disrupted, and ABC Sports suddenly had the responsibility of reporting a breaking news event to the world. Everyone gathered around their television sets, much as they would nearly three decades later on September 11, 2001—with one exception: *everyone was watching the same network.* Jim McKay was no longer a sports commentator but a news anchor with a grave assignment, and our tense, sixteen-hour broadcast would become a somber chapter in television history.

The Munich tragedy, like so many other events I witnessed and people I encountered during my voyage through global sport, filled me with a keen awareness that my colleagues and I were doing more than chronicling athletic achievements and creating travelogues. We were also expanding the American consciousness through the medium of television. By covering athletes as obscure as underhand block choppers and as famous as Olympic gymnasts, we learned that there was more to these athletes than competitive drive, more than simply the desire to win. Through them, we all felt an overriding sense of connection to one another and to the world. Just as on that summer day in Moscow in 1961, we saw rivals shake hands or embrace just moments after trying to vanquish each other. They seemed to walk away with an understanding that they were bound together for life by their experience, and those of us watching, whether from the booth, the stadium, or the couch, felt the same.

When *Wide World* returned to the airwaves in January 1962 after its first hiatus, it rolled out a new opening that became as famous as the show itself. Dramatic film clips of sporting triumphs and disasters were edited to a pulsating fanfare and a voice-over by Jim McKay:

> Spanning the globe to bring you the
> constant variety of sport
> The thrill of victory…and the agony of defeat
> The human drama of athletic competition
> This is *ABC's Wide World of Sports*!

Nearly every phrase Jim spoke in this opening became part of the American vernacular, and an unknown Slovenian ski jumper who lost his balance and veered off the ramp horrifically tumbled into fame as "the 'agony of defeat' guy."

For nearly forty years, *Wide World*'s ongoing cast of athletes would participate in more than 120 different sports in 58 different countries on five continents. The show's production values and style also carried over to ABC's ten Olympic telecasts between 1964 and 1988. All the world was, indeed, our stage, and the athletes our players. Watching their stories unfold, sometimes into legend, became a way of life for me for half a century. This book is my way of sharing the human drama of athletic competition.

2

Most Valuable Players

If you watched to the very end of one of ABC's later Olympic telecasts, you would have seen credits that seemed to run endlessly while hundreds of names scrolled, evidence of the massive coordination it took to televise such an event. One event alone could require more than twenty cameramen capturing the action, four video operators keeping the pictures clear and colors balanced, ten to twenty audio engineers riding microphones and pointing dishes, and a squad of videotape engineers cueing playback, billboards, profiles, and replays. The tip of this colossal iceberg of collaboration was displayed on a wall of about fifty monitors in front of flanks of producers, directors, and technical directors ready to launch the final package up to a satellite 24,000 miles out in space at the press of a button.

Whether we were putting together a fortnight of Olympic coverage or a weekly episode of *Wide World of Sports*, our ABC team consisted of two main men: Roone Arledge and Jim McKay. Roone was like the team owner, knowing when to be on the scene and when to just let his people do their thing. Jim was the star player, always in position to reach for that perfect pass and carry the ball over the goal line with incredible finesse.

ROONE PINCKNEY ARLEDGE JR.

The pews of St. Bartholomew's Church on Park Avenue were filled with just about every television notable you could imagine. ABC News anchor Barbara Walters concluded her remarks, followed by colleague Peter Jennings. Then a not-so-famous man took his place at the lectern. He was Richard "Dick" Wald, former president of NBC News and vice president at ABC News, then a professor of journalism at Columbia University. On that December day in 2002, Dick recalled that he first met the man we had gathered to remember while registering for classes at Columbia College in 1948. The lines were alphabetical, and in front of him was a guy with red hair and a big, round face. He pulled an empty curly pipe from his mouth and introduced himself as Roone Arledge.

"How do you do," Dick said. "Shouldn't you be in the *A* Line?"

"No," the cocksure Roone Arledge replied. "This line is shorter."

Dick awaited the inevitable comeuppance as Roone approached the registration table. There was a little shuffle, a "little buck-and-wing," and then the redhead with the unusual name left the table, registered.

"I knew at that moment," Dick said to the gathered mourners, "that I was in the presence of a truly great…pain in the ass!"

Those of us seated in the pews burst into laughter because we had all been frustrated in our dealings with Roone Arledge at one time or another. Still, there was something about this television sports and news giant that simply made things work. He was a visionary who knew how to be in charge without seeming to try, a leader who could maintain control even if his hands weren't on the wheel.

So, who was this guy? This Roone Pinckney Arledge Jr.?

In early 2011, I attended the annual scholarship ceremony at Columbia University because one of the awards was to be given in memory of my wife Betsy's uncle, Professor George W. Hibbitt. The ceremony took place in the Roone Arledge Auditorium—but, to my surprise, neither the recipient of the Hibbitt scholarship nor any of the other brilliant young minds seated at our table had a clue as to who the facility's namesake was.

"He's the man who created *Monday Night Football!*" I exclaimed to the youngsters. "He developed *Wide World of Sports*, the diving board from which all television sports programming sprang! He turned the Olympics into a world television event and trained just about everyone who runs today's broadcast entities, ESPN, NBC, CBS, and Fox!"

The undergraduates' eyes widened. They leaned in, as if they were my grandchildren gathering 'round to hear a really good story. I told them that for the last half of the twentieth century, the name Roone Arledge was a household word. Week after week, from 1961 through 1988, millions of Americans heard the words, "The executive producer of *ABC's Wide World of Sports* is Roone Arledge." This mantra was repeated at the end of NBA telecasts, *The American Sportsman*, the *Professional Bowlers Tour*, and of course, *Monday Night Football*, which consistently ranked in the top-ten television shows.

Roone was my boss for twenty-five years. He was drolly brilliant—a guy who carried a full beverage glass in each hand at any gathering so that if someone stopped him with whom he did not care to converse, he simply told that person that someone else was waiting for his drink and moved on. Relentless in his pursuit of excellence, Roone professed to those of us in his employ what he called The Second Steak Theory. He noted that when you order a steak in a restaurant medium rare and it arrives well done, you call the waiter over and send it back. But no one ever sends back the second steak! The second steak isn't really about the steak; it's about the principle. You've given an order, and the people serving you have acquiesced to your demands. You're the king. Even if the second steak arrives undercooked, you will eat it. For Roone, it was always about the steak. If he wanted a clip reedited, for example, he would look at the new version with the same critical eye he used the first time around because nothing guaranteed that the revision would be any better than the original.

Roone also knew the dramatic effect of storytelling and immediacy. He believed that intrinsic to covering an event was to show not only the competition but also what it was like to be there, a novel idea at the time. In 1973, I was a spectator when *Wide World* televised a boxing match from Monaco. After the broadcast, Roone barked that the fight might as well have taken place in old St. Nick's Arena on West Sixty-Sixth for all the audience would know. Behind the outdoor ring, in full view, was the Prince's Palace towering above the sparkling city-state on the French Riviera—and no one at home ever saw it! Roone used the incident to reemphasize our standard procedure: go outside, capture the atmosphere of the location, and make it a part of the presentation. In other words, make the viewers feel as if they have been yanked off the couch, given a personal tour of the place, taken into the locker room to meet the athletes, and then plopped into a front row seat.

As for Roone's management style, producer/director Chet Forte once said it was "all effed up, but it worked." Part of Roone's methodology was to give free hand to producers and directors so we could be as creative as each of us was capable of being. He seldom complimented us, however, which gave the environment in which we worked a certain air of insecurity. If we received a note that said "Well done" or "Nice job" with a scribbled "R," we considered it a huge compliment.

Roone Arledge did things his way, and we producers were to do the same, especially in the early days when we never had to worry about budgets. We always did a site survey prior to an event to figure out what was needed for optimal coverage—a camera here, a camera there, a platform here, a crane there. If a wild camera position would require approval from the event organizers and installing it might also interrupt a practice schedule, Roone expected us to go for it anyway. On one occasion, I wanted to use a Houston Crane for a camera position and anticipated certain refusal by officials. "Of course they will," Roone said. "Then you sit down and talk about it." We got the crane.

Roone had deep insight into human nature and knew that everything was negotiable. He recognized that people tend to be resistant to change and new ideas, but he also respected boundaries. He would never ask for anything that would distract or endanger athletes or that might interrupt an event.

To watch the man in action was to learn his methods. When we returned to New York from the Mexico City Olympics in a torrential rain, it was cold and virtually impossible to get a cab. Drivers who got dragged all the way out to JFK from Manhattan wanted a decent fare back. After several taxis drove by ignoring him, Roone shouted "Westchester!" at one of them, and the cab stopped immediately. Once his secretary, Vicki Brawn, was settled in the backseat, Roone told the driver to take her to Woodside, which was just minutes away. The cabbie protested, and I stood in awe as Roone simply repeated the driver's cab number over and over until the driver understood that he would be reported if he didn't take Vicki home—and do so with civility.

There evolved, very early on, an omnipresent quality to Roone's leadership, yet he managed to be elusive. He was notorious for not returning phone calls. Rumor had it that at the end of the day, all the telephone message slips that had piled up on the corner of his desk were swept off the edge into a wastebasket. When he became president of ABC News in addition to being president of ABC Sports, we joked that now he had two offices where you wouldn't be able to reach him. My office was only forty feet from his on the twenty-eighth floor at ABC headquarters in New York, yet I still had trouble getting hold of him. One evening, after he had ignored my messages for ten weeks, I resorted to waiting outside his office. At last, he emerged.

"If you want to see me," he said, pausing, "just pop your head through the doorway sometime."

He was halfway to the elevators before I could utter a word.

Roone showed up for events only when he felt his presence was required and often changed plans at the last minute. By doing so, he created a sort of mystique about himself. Looking back, I assume Roone had to maintain some sense of focus to successfully run the divisions, or perhaps it was his other doctrine, The Tyranny of the Telephone. Roone felt no requirement to answer a phone. It rudely interrupts. It disengages you from what you've decided is your priority at the moment, whether it's a work project or a family dinner. When you answer a phone, you are reacting to what someone else wants, and Roone Arledge was anything but reactive. I can only wonder what he would think of today's additional intrusions, where that annoying phone is now "smart" and ringing in your pocket! Would we be hearing about the Tyranny of the Tweet?

One evening in 1977, Roone called me into his office after business hours. He poured me a glass of scotch and asked me what my ambitions were. Ultimately, our conversation shifted to him. After his extraordinary leadership during the 1972 Munich Olympic tragedy, Roone's reputation took a major leap. Now he was being encouraged to expand into entertainment or possibly news. We talked about it all for nearly three hours. Then, standing on the corner of Fifty-Fourth Street and Avenue of the Americas about to go our separate ways, Roone asked me what I thought he should do.

I was flattered he even cared what I thought.

"Would you rather be involved with the life and times of *Laverne and Shirley*," I asked, referring to the hit sitcom at the time, "or would you rather cover significant historic events?"

Later that year, Roone became president of ABC News in addition to continuing as president of the sports division. ABC News ranked third in the ratings behind CBS and NBC, so Roone had his work cut out for him. He went on to create *Nightline, World News Tonight, 20/20, Primetime Live,* and *This Week with David Brinkley*. He also turned Peter Jennings, Barbara Walters, Ted Koppel, and Diane Sawyer into television news icons and took the network to the number one spot.

Although I can't take credit for nudging Roone into broadcast news, I do like to think that—at least for a few moments on a New York City sidewalk—I made a difference to Roone Pinckney Arledge Jr.

JIM MCKAY

Jim McKay was the consummate journalist, but he didn't come across as a TV anchor in the paternal way that Walter Cronkite did. Jim came into our living rooms more like a good friend, the guy next door, your favorite uncle, who was eager to tell you all about where he was and what he was witnessing. This feeling of intimacy may have been the result of some advice Jim told me he had received while working at CBS in the 1950s. Arthur Godfrey, the most prominent name in broadcasting at the time, told Jim that when he talked into a camera, he should talk to only one person. So the millions of people who watched Jim McKay host thirty-seven years of *Wide World of Sports* and ten Olympic Games, had no idea that they were eavesdropping on Jim's conversations with his wife, Margaret.

There was a wide-eyed wonder to Jim's delivery, especially in the early years of *Wide World*. He was a "Connecticut Yankee" reveling in the court of world-class sports competition. He presented a charming "innocents abroad" quality, so to speak. Jim had never been to Europe, so as we journeyed from city to city, he was taking it all in for the first time himself and savoring the adventures right alongside the viewers. He also possessed a sensitivity to what he was experiencing or witnessing vis-à-vis his role as host. He knew that the sporting events we were covering could not be separated from the world around them or from society in general.

The 1973 World Table Tennis Championship in Sarajevo, then a city in the now bygone Socialist Federal Republic of Yugoslavia, was a prime example. The competition took place only a few months after the Munich Massacre, so the aftermath of that tragedy weighed heavily on our minds. Yugoslavia seemed a world away from more familiar Western Europe, and these championships included countries that were not yet even participating in the Olympics—including China, a table tennis powerhouse, and countries in the Middle East. Sitting in the lobby of our hotel, sipping syrup-thick coffee, our lungs filling with the sickly sweet smells of exotic eastern tobaccos, it wasn't so much the scents of Sarajevo that intrigued us as it was the sounds. Sounds made for impressive scene sets, so we opened this one with the distinct cry of an imam's call to prayer and the image of an ancient minaret towering over a Muslim mosque, then pulled back to a wide shot of the misty city from a nearby mountainside. Then multiple calls from multiple mosques clashed with the ringing bells of Greek Orthodox churches. As the dissonance crescendoed, Jim spoke about the assassination of Archduke Ferdinand of Austria, which took place in Sarajevo and sparked the chain of events that led to the outbreak of the First World War. We then entered a bazaar and moved down a back alley Jim described as being a place where one might see the ghosts of Sydney Greenstreet and Peter Lorre looking for the icon with the stolen jewels in *Casablanca*. And, finally, the popping of Ping-Pong balls overrode the bells as the television picture panned the international flags flying outside the arena, then dissolved inside to a single table, pulling out to reveal action on sixteen tables in two rows, bringing the scene set to a cacophonous conclusion.

Jim and I were quite proud of that collaboration. It clearly reflected Sarajevo's tumultuous history of multiethnic and religious conflict that, unfortunately, resurfaced in the 1990s. The segment was also a perfect example of Jim's master storytelling and keen sense of dramatic structure. These qualities were what made him so good at connecting history with sporting events—*and* connecting with his audience.

Those of us on the ABC crew lived our careers in the reflected glory of Jim's words. He put the verbal frosting on our production cake and always brought our work to a higher level, whether it was for a Formula One Grand Prix or a wrist-wrestling championship. And he did it like no other because, in addition to being a journalist, a storyteller, and a history teacher, Jim McKay was also a poet.

For our 1971 telecast of the Calgary Stampede, Canada's famed rodeo/ national country fair, we filmed wild horses from a helicopter as they galloped across the prairie, then chased a streamliner train racing along a riverbed toward the city skyline. I then added the swirling, big-sky theme music from the classic western *The Big Country* to the soundtrack. After editing, Jim came in to do the narration, which he always wrote himself. He viewed the video twice, asked a few questions about timing, then told us that he'd be down the hall and to join him in about fifteen minutes. When we did, Jim took his seat in the announce booth. We rolled tape and cued the music, then Jim:

> *The ranches are quiet where the dirt roads lead*
> *Everybody's goin' to the great Stampede...*

Jim hadn't written commentary, he had written a poem! As the wild horses and train bolted across the monitor, Jim's verse moved along with them.

> *And they come to the town in a silver steed*
> *The great train headed for the great Stampede...*

When Jim died in 2008, his son, Sean McManus, the president of CBS News and Sports at the time, asked me to speak at the funeral. It was, and remains, as high an honor as any in my life. Sean was adamant that I limit my talk to five minutes, which was such a challenge when talking about Jim McKay. The one story that came to mind was a bit chancy, but it always amused me when I thought about it—and no one had heard it before.

On the day of the service, I nervously walked toward the altar of the cavernous Cathedral of St. Mary the Queen in Baltimore. My eyes met Margaret's, and the anxiety melted away. We touched hands, and as I proceeded up the steps to the lectern, I thought, "It's OK. I'm just talking to Margaret."

I looked at her, then over the crowd.

"It's time for a confession."

There was a stunning moment of silence.

"And what could be a more appropriate place for it than in this beautiful cathedral?"

Margaret turned pale.

I told the mourners that it had to do with a certain automobile ride in France when Jim and I were returning from the Le Mans race on our way to the airport in Paris. We had stopped at a quaint roadside bistro for some cheese and a fine bottle of Beaujolais-Villages. Well satisfied and ready to complete our journey, Jim donned his leather driving gloves with a flare and got behind the wheel of our rented BMW. As we exited the parking lot, a black Mercedes cut us off and turned toward Paris.

With the roar of the race cars apparently still pulsating through his veins, Jim put the pedal to the metal. It was like watching Snoopy come down from the roof of his doghouse and morph into a Formula One driver. No doubt the Red Baron himself was at the wheel of the Mercedes, and Jim was determined to pass that black menace one way or another.

For about thirty kilometers we raced across the French countryside, but Jim couldn't do it. He'd find an opening and then suddenly a chicane or a curve or a narrowing of the road would force him to back off. With about a half mile to go, there was a straightaway. Jim pulled into the left lane, floored his ultimate driving machine, and whizzed past the Mercedes for the checkered flag.

He pulled into the airport as if it were a victory lane. With the car at the curb, Jim stood, champion of all he surveyed. He removed his driving gloves finger by finger, then slapped them into his left hand. His victory speech consisted of just three words.

"Don't…tell…Margaret!"

3

The Greatest

I saw a kaleidoscope of athletes while working at ABC Sports, but how to pick one standout from a cast of thousands? Sports fans are always verbally jousting over that question. When Michael Phelps won his twenty-second medal in swimming at the London Olympics in 2012, sports commentators and fans everywhere debated the question once again. Should the title of "The World's Greatest Athlete" be bestowed on he who has won the most Olympic medals? Or should it go instead to someone who has dominated her sport for decades, such as another London Olympian, Kimberly Rhode, who won her fifth consecutive Olympic gold in skeet shooting? Or does the title go to its traditional bearer, the Olympic decathlon champion—someone like Jim Thorpe, who not only won the 1912 decathlon and pentathlon but also played professional football, basketball, and baseball?

The gibber-gabber over the answer to this question is always fun, but always inconclusive. Still, three athletes come to mind when I am asked. Two of them told everyone that they were, in fact, the greatest...the third, a rather shy young girl, completely *devoted* herself to greatness.

ALI

Miami, 1964. Don Dunphy, the "Voice of Boxing," the man who delivered the blow-by-blow coverage of most of the celebrated boxing matches of the mid-twentieth century, was in town to cover a fight. As we passed through a low-ceilinged hallway on our way into the arena, a beautiful young man blocked the entrance. His shoes were smooth white high-tops, the kind boxers wore. His body was lengthy and lithe, draped in off-white trousers and shirt; his face boyish, yet strikingly handsome; his attitude, proud and braggadocian. He told Dunphy about his prowess and that one day he would be heavyweight champion of the world. He then made sure that Dunphy knew when his next fight was. Gracious and smiling, Dunphy told the young man he would be watching. I thought to myself, *Who is this guy?*

He was Cassius Marcellus Clay.

Clay, who would change his name to Muhammad Ali when he joined the Nation of Islam in 1964, not only became heavyweight champion of the world but also the most famous athlete, if not person, on the planet. His fame transcended sports, and he became a historic figure with regard to social, religious, and civil rights issues. Whether I agreed with all he did or not, for me, Muhammad Ali was the most important athlete of the twentieth century.

Ali was always controversial. That was part of his appeal. He was brash and cocky, and he had a big mouth. He made predictions about knocking out opponents. He taunted them and gave them nicknames. In 1975, he said of rival Joe Frazier, "It'll be a killa, a chilla, a thrilla, when I get the gorilla in Manila." Before his first heavyweight championship fight in 1964, Clay called Sonny Liston "the Big Ugly Bear." Liston was considered to be indomitable—he was big, tough, and had a sinister, frightening look about him. Many thought Clay would be destroyed. Instead he became world champion, announced that he had changed his name to Muhammad Ali, and declared himself "king of the world."

Ali quickly became the controversial talk of the nation.

Even before the Iranian hostage crisis of 1979, the 1993 bombing of the World Trade Center in New York, and the September 11, 2001 terrorist attacks, changing your name and announcing that you had become a Muslim was still an unpopular move in the United States. In general, folks wanted their heavyweight champions, especially if they were black, to be in the image of Joe Louis, who voluntarily enlisted in the army during World War II and served his country in harmony with the patriotism of that time. Not Ali. He marched to a different drummer. In 1967, he refused to be inducted into the US Army based on his religious beliefs and famously stated, "I ain't got no quarrel with them Viet Cong…no Viet Cong ever called me nigger." Ali was arrested, vilified in the press, stripped of his world title and boxing license, and convicted of draft evasion. As one of the first national figures to speak out against the war, Ali's message and attitude resonated with a lot of young Americans in the growing counterculture of the late 1960s.

One of the very few sports figures who openly supported Ali during this time was another celebrity of controversy, ABC commentator Howard Cosell. Howard Cosell was one of a kind. In a 1970 *TV Guide* poll, he was voted the most popular—*and* the least popular—sportscaster in the country. He delivered brilliant commentary with the haughty vocabulary and style of an Englishman, but in a Brooklyn accent with a distinct staccato cadence. Like Ali, Cosell always stirred the pot. He slammed announcers who were employed by the ball clubs, saying they were devoid of journalistic integrity, and he despised "expert commentators"—retired athletes who transitioned to the broadcast booth—calling such a practice "jockocracy." Voicing his opinions didn't exactly endear Cosell to either team owners or his fellow broadcasters.

Although many broadcasters of the era continued to call Ali by his former name, Cosell defended Ali on the air in 1967. The one-time lawyer opined that the young fighter had the constitutional right to change his name and refuse the draft, whether people agreed with it or not and liked it or not. What made Cosell's statements even more provocative was that he was Jewish.

So began a relationship between Cosell and Ali that millions of television viewers savored telecast after telecast. Cosell once referred to their interviews as sparring sessions. Their rapport was, indeed, peculiar, but beyond the on-air shtick, it was clear the two had a deep, mutual respect. They also understood how they played off each other—Cosell with calculation and Ali with instinct. In 1967, for example, when Cosell asked Ali if he was taking opponent Zora Folley too lightly, Ali interrupted him and jabbered, "I'm confident I'll whip all of 'em. This ain't nothin' new. My image has been confidence. What you trying to make it look like somethin' new for? I'm always confident I'll whip all of them!" "You're being extremely truculent," Cosell said sarcastically. To which Ali replied, "Whatever truculent means, if it's good, I'm that!"

Ali appealed his draft evasion conviction all the way to the Supreme Court, which overturned the lower court's ruling. When his three-year banishment from fighting was lifted, Ali was set to fight Jerry Quarry in October of 1970. Naturally, there was a lot of press over the return of the man who had spent some of the prime years of his fighting career in boxing exile. To me, especially with the Vietnam War still in progress, the bout with Quarry was much more than just a boxing match. It was a demonstration of civil rights. A man who had been cut off at the knees for standing up for his beliefs—an Olympic gold medalist who had been refused service in a restaurant because of the color of his skin—was back on his feet in the ring. Ali vs. Quarry was, indeed, a heavyweight battle. It was a black man from Louisville, Kentucky, fighting a white man from Bellflower, California, in Atlanta, Georgia.

The event produced a lot of security concerns. The crowd included Lester Maddox, then governor of Georgia and a staunch segregationist, and what *Sports Illustrated* described as "the most startling assembly of black power and black money ever displayed." Contrasting styles were also on display in the ring. For one, Ali didn't always hold up his gloves in the typical boxing stance. I think this enabled him to rest his arms. Second, he moved with such fluidity, such elastic grace and speed, that Quarry, or any opponent, had great difficulty reaching him. Ali never got close to Quarry for more than an instant and never provided a stable target. His anticipation was so keen that he was already moving backward when punches came his way. While Ali did his unique dance and dodge, Quarry did the classic bob and weave, becoming the center of a pugilistic wagon wheel. Ali was the rim, constantly circling Quarry clockwise, jabbing, jabbing with his left to set up that devastating right. In the middle of the third round, one of those rights opened a deep cut over Quarry's left eye. His team attended to the wound during the break. "The Bellflower Bomber" defiantly jumped up to start the fourth round, but after a doctor took a look, the fight was stopped.

ABC planned to air the bout the following Saturday afternoon on *Wide World of Sports*. As producer of the telecast, I wanted Ali to come into the studio to review the video with Cosell and analyze the fight. During a telephone conversation with one of Ali's representatives to hammer out the details, the young man started pressing for all kinds of extras for an entourage, including airfare, limos, and the like. I grew concerned that I wouldn't close the deal. Then Ali came back on the line. He was clearly embarrassed and told me that the man with whom I had been speaking was new and that he had put him on the line to give him some experience talking to the network. Ali then expressed his deep sense of gratitude toward Cosell and ABC and said, "If you need me in New York on Thursday, I'll be there."

His words were so unexpected and so meaningful because all I had seen of Muhammad Ali through the years was the showman, the show-off, the braggart, the man who inherently knew that saying outrageous things would help carve him a unique place in boxing history. But on that day, I experienced a sensitive and sincere side of the man that he had seldom, if ever, revealed to the public.

Years later, in 1986, as I was preparing for the production of the prime-time special celebrating the twenty-fifth anniversary of *ABC's Wide World of Sports*, another incident took place that verified the depth of Ali's human spirit. More than fifty of the century's greatest athletes flew to New York to be part of the program. Ali and motorcycle dare-devil Evel Knievel were among them, but my plan was to hold them in the green room until later in the show to raise the level of audience response. Evel's appearances on *Wide World* accounted for seven of the show's ten highest-rated programs, and Ali headlined the remaining three.

Three days before the taping, Ali phoned me. He was upset about not being able to sit with the other audience members throughout the show. "I want to be with the people," he said. I asked if he would come to the studio the next day during our lunch break so we could talk about it.

As I stood in ABC's TV-1 Studio on West Sixty-Sixth waiting for Ali, I looked around and thought about all the television history that had taken place in that space. To think what started as an indoor horseback-riding arena would become the site of the first televised presidential debate, the crucial Kennedy/Nixon contest in 1960. While I was waiting, the only other person in the studio at the time was Bob Marr, the head property man. A lone work light cast a quiet glow over the *Wide World* crest, which had just been painted on the floor. I felt a tug on my ear, spun around, and there was that face again. The one I had first seen in Miami. Still handsome, but no longer boyish.

"Yes, it's me. It's me," Ali said with a disarming smile.

I noticed his speech had slowed. He had recently been diagnosed with Parkinson's disease, and the resulting loss of muscle function was starting to show. His mind remained sharp as ever, though. He was accompanied by his brother, Rahman Ali, and manager Jabir Herbert Muhammad, the son of Nation of Islam founder Wallace Fard Muhammad. Before we started, Bob handed Ali a large art card and asked him for his autograph. Ali stepped away and placed the card on top of a packing crate. I was disheartened as I watched him write because he seemed to take an inordinate amount of time to sign his name. The grace and agility he had shown "dancing like a butterfly and stinging like a bee" had faded.

Ali handed the card to Bob and returned to the group. I explained to Ali that because he had appeared on *Wide World* more than any other athlete (over seventy times!), he would be the climax of the two-hour special. A twelve-minute video about him would be shown to the audience in the darkened studio, and then he would be revealed on stage. Being a showman himself, Ali understood. I then directed Ali to move downstage where he would greet Jim McKay. I took his hand as Jim would and said, "And Jim will probably say, 'Muhammad, you are the greatest.'"

"You just findin' that out!" he quipped.

After Ali departed, Bob walked over to me and handed me the art card. I was wrong about why Ali had taken so long. He did more than sign his name:

> Service to others is the rent we pay for our room in
> the Hereafter.
>
> —Muhammad Ali

The anniversary show went flawlessly. After the final credits rolled, I hastily left the control room to look for Ali on the studio floor to thank him. I moved through the crowd and found him in the center, standing on the *Wide World of Sports* crest. I was about to speak, when he said, "I just want to thank you for all you did for me tonight." Then I felt his heavyweight champion arms embrace me.

EVEL

"I don't do takes!" Evel Knievel screamed at me. "I'm not an actor. What I do is real, and you get it when I do it, or you don't get it at all!"

The superstar daredevil of the 1970s had just left his London hotel and stopped to sign autographs for the kids waiting for him. Evel was in the UK to jump thirteen double-decker buses in Wembley Stadium on a motorcycle. I was following him with a camera crew for *Wide World* and wasn't completely happy with what I saw being taped. I made the mistake of asking Evel to go back inside the hotel and do it all again.

Not a chance.

Robert Craig Knievel Jr. was a consummate performer and a marketing genius. This wild-western mountain-boy dreamer from Butte, Montana, had created a character named Evel Knievel and played the part to perfection, right down to the star-spangled leather suit. He was an "Elvis on wheels" who risked life and limb while leaping over buses, canyons, and rattlesnakes. The jumps were no act, however. He used no gimmicks and no trickery, as evidenced by the Guinness World Record he holds for most broken bones in a lifetime.

The man who inspired what we now call extreme sports definitely did things his way, even before he became a household name. When I stood with him overlooking the gaping, mile-wide pit that was the Anaconda Copper Mine in which he once worked, Evel pointed to the depths below and a lineup of huge loading trucks with six-foot-high wheels. He used to drive one of those trucks, and they would all line up in the open mine and, in turn, pick up a giant load of copper ore, unload it into a railroad car, and rejoin the line. Evel told me that the foreman had always had a grudge against him for some reason. One day, he warned Evel that he was keeping an eye on him and that he had better not screw up. In the next go-round, Evel loaded up and, as he passed the foreman's shack, he pulled out of line and dumped the whole load on top of the shack…burying it. He then drove the truck to the middle of downtown Butte, went into a bar, and waited to get arrested.

So the legend goes.

Evel tended to color any story he told as part of his act, but I always felt there was truth at the core. After he became famous and sought frontier justice on someone who had done him wrong, it was easy to believe the hyperbole. That someone was producer/writer Sheldon Saltman, who became involved in Evel's Snake River Canyon jump in Idaho in 1974. Evel grew to think of Saltman as a friend—until Saltman wrote a book about the experience called *Evel Knievel on Tour*. Evel was not happy about some of the things said about him, so he painted a baseball bat red, white, and blue, waited for Saltman in the 20th Century Fox parking lot, and beat the hell out of him. When his lawyers pleaded "not guilty" in court, Evel interrupted them, fired them, and said he did it and would do it again. Evel ended up in jail but was lucky that was all that happened to him.

After his unsuccessful attempt to propel himself over the Snake River Canyon in a steam-powered, bullet-shaped vehicle called the Skycycle in 1974, Evel signed with British producers/promoters John Daly and David Hemmings to begin a world tour. London was the first stop. Evel arrived about three weeks before the jump and was shocked to learn that only 3,000 tickets had been sold for the 100,000-seat Wembley Stadium. When I arrived in London later, everyone was abuzz over the stir Evel caused at his first press conference, which was held at the airport. Evel told me that he publicly fired a couple of his promotion guys, then said to the reporters, "I'm very glad to be here in England, where we came and won the war for yah!"

Pencils began scratching briskly across their pads. This guy was outrageous, perfect fodder for the British tabloids—and he was clearly orchestrating the entire spectacle. For his next act, the greatest barnstormer of the twentieth century arranged to have his customized, chrome-plated, 1974 Cadillac pickup truck delivered to London. We followed with our cameras as Evel donned his star-spangled suit and simply drove through London where his "blood-red Batmobile-cum-aircraft carrier-sized Cadillac," as one reporter described it, stood out among the black cabs and drab buildings. The *Daily Mirror* journalist who tagged along for a "ride on the wild side" wrote that Evel switched lanes like a Formula One driver, rounded corners glued to the curb, and missed everything by half an inch. "I've never had an accident in an automobile, only on motorcycles," Evil assured him. When stopped at traffic lights, Evel hung out the window and talked to people on the sidewalks, especially the kids. He gestured them to approach the car, asked their names and whether they wore helmets when they rode their bikes. A few days later, while sitting in the bar at the Tower Hotel next to London Bridge, I listened as Evel bet a man he could hit a golf ball across the Thames. He also made sure that nearby reporters heard the wager. Evel had me go to his room to fetch his driver from his golf bag and a bath mat so he could tee up on the cement parapet at river's edge. The Thames was much wider than even a pro golfer could clear. Nonetheless, Evel kept trying, and the sight of him driving golf balls off the hotel promenade garnered him yet more media attention.

The second press conference was held on live TV and was just as entertaining as his media stunts around the city. I wasn't there, but my colleagues told me that toward the end, a little lady from the BBC raised her hand and in lilting, proper English said, "Mistah Knievel, don't you think that your failiah to jump the Snake River Canyon has damaged your credibility?" Without pause, Evel replied, "No canyon, and no woman, I ever jumped, ever damaged my credibility."

Then Evel hired the premier English photographer Harry Ormesher to do a photo shoot, for which Evel arranged to have thirteen London buses set up in a parking lot. When Harry returned from the shoot, he shook his head and said to me, "You are not going to believe this." He told me that when he arrived on scene, he began to discuss with Evel where he wanted him to stand and the various angles he planned to shoot. But Evel made it clear that Harry would shoot just *one* picture. He also threatened to fire Harry unless he followed instructions. Evel told Harry that he, Evel, would stand centered and that Harry was to go out at a ninety-degree angle far enough to get all of the busses in frame with a wide-angle lens. Evel knew there was only one way a newspaper could print such a picture: *all the way across the page*!

About an hour before the jump, football-star-turned-commentator Frank Gifford and I visited Evel while he rested in his trailer, which was on display on the hallowed Wembley turf along with the broken Skycycle. The stadium was already starting to fill, and Evel was a bit weary from a late night of barhopping. I noticed the bottle of Wild Turkey within reach and the ever-present aspirin to ease the pain of broken bones, calcium deposits, and arthritis. Evel reclined on a couch, with his shorter leg (the price of his calamitous Caesar's Palace jump in 1967) raised and resting on the arm. "There are more people in this Wembley Stadium than in my hometown of Butte, Montana," he remarked. I would not learn until I returned to the United States that Evel had shared with Frank the night before that he knew he wouldn't make it over the thirteenth bus. He claimed that the proper gearbox for his cycle had not yet arrived. Weeks later when I asked him why he didn't remove a bus, he looked at me with disbelief and reminded me that he was the world's greatest daredevil. He asked me to just imagine if he had walked up the ramp and told eighty thousand people that he had to take away a bus because a gearbox hadn't arrived from New Jersey!

Evel knew who he was and what he had to do—at all times—including when he didn't make it over that last bus and crashed. I knew what I had to do, too. As director, I had to be sure that we were ready for all outcomes. If the jump didn't go well, I would not be able to rely on the TV coverage or a handheld mike, so I made sure a tiny tape recorder, called a Mini Nagra, was planted on Frank.

Evel warmed up one bike, didn't like the gearing, switched to another, and made a practice run down the approach ramp that started in the second tier of bleachers. The crowd jeered a bit as Evel headed back to the top of the ramp, where he gave a thumbs-up and made some quick, final checks on the bike. Then he revved the engine, and off he went, reaching ninety miles an hour before he was airborne. Sure enough, he landed one bus short and was catapulted forward, tumbling across the ground before finally resting at the other end of the stadium floor, the bike settling atop his legs. Frank dropped his role as commentator and rushed to his friend's side. The Mini Nagra picked up Evel telling Frank that he wanted to be lifted from the stretcher and helped up the ramp so he could address the crowd. Frank tried to talk him out of it, but Evel insisted. Once atop the buses, a dazed Evel spoke haltingly: "Ladies and Gentlemen of this wonderful country, I've got to tell you that you are the last people in the world who will ever see me jump because I will never ever, ever jump again. I'm through." He then insisted on walking out on his own two feet, though he was barely able to maintain an upright position on the shoulders of Frank and another man. Frank kept trying to convince Evel to lie on the stretcher, as he had already proved enough, but Evel begged, "I want to walk out of this stadium...Please let me walk out. Help me out, Frank." Frank relented, and the eighty thousand English men and women shouted, "Hip, hip, hooray! Hip, hip, hooray!" The banged-up and already bruising, dauntless performer paused to wave with his good arm.

A few days later, I was back in New York to edit the footage for our weekend broadcast. At 5:30 a.m., the phone rang at my bedside. It was Evel calling from his hospital bed in London, where he was nursing a broken pelvis, broken hand, and fractured vertebra. He told me not to use the quote about retiring in our *Wide World* telecast. When I asked him why, he said because he might jump again and didn't want kids to think he was a liar. I told him that everyone would understand, that he was in shock after his crash, and no one would blame him for his emotional state. Evel then threatened to sue me and ABC and hung up.

Evel Knievel wasn't one to ever say "I'm sorry," but he apologized in his own way. After our airing of his London spree and the Wembley jump, which became a *Wide World of Sports* Top Ten, Evel gave me his practice helmet, on which he had signed, "To Doug, Your pal, Evel."

Evel called himself "a professional life risker," and five months later, despite his doctor's warnings that even the slightest trauma could sever his damaged spinal cord and paralyze him, the indestructible one was back. I was dispatched to Butte to film material for ABC's prime-time special "Evel Knievel—Portrait of a Daredevil," which would air a few weeks before his jump at Kings Island, Ohio, in October of 1975. This jump would become the highest-rated episode of *Wide World* ever—even outshining

Muhammad Ali and George Foreman's "Rumble in the Jungle"—and my visit to Butte would give me a taste of the high life, Evel style.

On a sunny day in August 1975, Evel led me, cameraman Don Shoemaker, and soundman Jimmy Williams to a one-story stone building in Butte. The former miner, who never formally graduated from high school, now had himself an office building! With hometown pride, he pointed out that the building was constructed of rock culled from the surrounding Rocky Mountains. The structure wasn't huge—the footprint was only about eighty by fifty feet—and its light-colored stone made it sparkle in the sunlight.

Evel swung the front door open with a flourish and invited us in. The main room was quite simple. A long bar, looking well stocked and well used, paralleled the far wall, and posters and artwork celebrating his storied career decorated the room. To the right was a freestanding, full-size, solid steel bank vault, complete with one of those imposing large stainless-steel wheels. It seemed that the whole purpose of the building was to house this multiton lockbox.

Evel informed us that the vault was on a timer, so the window of entry was limited. The time was now. With the flair of a showman, the man who bragged about being a safecracker and bank robber earlier in life, turned the wheel and dramatically pulled open the huge metal door, revealing a full-size Harley-Davidson motorcycle…plated in gold! In order for us to fully appreciate Evel's prized possession, however, he first had to brush away the loose cash that had been "deposited" all over it like confetti. We could only surmise that this vault was Evel's personal piggy bank.

Evel had a curious relationship with money and talked about it often as part of his shtick. "All the money in the world can't buy your way into heaven," I heard him say once. "Can't buy your way out of hell. It was made to be spent right here, and I'm going to have the best clothes, best boots, best diamonds, best cars, trucks, motorcycles, booze, and women on the face of this earth just as long as I can keep going." He didn't believe in saving money, either. "If God wanted us to save [money], he'd of put handles on it so you could carry it around." Years later, when Evel ran into trouble with the IRS, I was not surprised.

After we finished beholding the Golden Hog, Evel muscled the foot-thick door back into place, turned the wheel into lock position, and told us it couldn't be opened again until the timer system recycled. We repaired to the bar where our host served up some beer, then left to tend to something in the adjacent storage room. As Don, Jimmy, and I enjoyed our cold ones, we conspired to play a joke on the ultimate jokester.

Whenever Evel oversaw the construction of an approach ramp for one of his stunts, he was obsessed with one thing: lining everything up with intense precision—straight lines and perfect angles. Each ramp was meticulously set and inspected and reinspected repeatedly because even the slightest offset could result in the motorcycle flying off course with devastating results. So, while Evel busied himself in the next room, Don, Jimmy, and I went around the main room and set each of the framed pictures slightly askew. We then rushed back to our barstools and waited.

After returning to the room, Evel quickly became distracted. We all kept straight faces while he looked around the room trying to figure it out. Then he saw the tilted pictures.

"Who did it?…Who did it?!"

He comically sounded like James Cagney as Captain Morton in *Mister Roberts* when he discovers that his pet palm tree has been thrown overboard. Evel then darted to the far corner and worked his way around the room, obsessively realigning each picture.

Thirty years later, Evel's health was sadly in decline, and he wanted to make amends to those he had treated badly. Prior to that time, Evel had amusingly recalled to me conversations he had had with Kathy Lee Gifford, the talk show host and Frank's wife, wherein the devout Christian would talk endlessly about the Lord to the point of driving Evel nuts. On one occasion, Evel told me he started a conversation with Kathy Lee with "I hate Jesus!" just for kicks. But seven months before he died in 2007, Evel was baptized by televangelist and pastor Dr. Robert Schuller during his *Hour of Power* telecast from the Crystal Cathedral in Garden Grove, California. Even Evel's baptism was a spectacle. Afterward, he called and proudly told me it was the largest crowd the mega-church ever had, with people lined up outside. He was as excited as if he had just cleared the Grand Canyon and had been welcomed on the other side by cheering throngs.

Evel's leap of faith was deep and sincere. It was as though he had taken a good look at those slightly askew frames of his life—the philandering, the hard drinking, the opulent lifestyle, the reckless behavior—and tried, albeit late, to straighten them all out.

NADIA

She pushed open the glass door of the space-age Pan Am Worldport at John F. Kennedy International Airport to face a room full of newspeople, policemen, government officials, and television cameras. For her, it literally was landing in another world. The twenty-eight-year-old looked fatigued but was smiling. I was the first person she recognized, and she walked straight toward me. While we hugged, I slipped a folded piece of paper with my phone numbers on it into her hand. Before we had a chance to speak, she was whisked away and guided toward a riser.

"Who are you?" a reporter standing next to me asked.

"A friend," I replied. I then looked up to a podium, where the young woman stood defenselessly before a cluster of microphones and shouting reporters.

Welcome to New York. December 1, 1989.

Nadia Comaneci, World and Olympic gymnastics champion, darling of the 1976 Games in Montreal, had defected from her native Romania, where a bloody revolution would take place just weeks later, deposing the country's longtime communist dictator, Nicolae Ceauşescu.

Inside the Pan Am terminal, Nadia faced the usual, uncontrolled shouts of members of the press. I could not understand why someone was not helping her. Her command of English was weak then, and she was exhausted from a harrowing Von-Trapp-like nighttime escape into Hungary, another communist country. After slipping away from Hungarian police, she and the other fugitives were driven six hours and dropped off near the Austrian border, where they trudged through thigh-high icy water, then climbed over seven barbed-wire fences. Bloodied, but relieved, they finally stepped into Austria and freedom. The next day she walked into the US Embassy and declared she wanted to go to America. Two hours later Nadia was aboard a jet christened "The Liberty Bell" and on her way. There in the terminal, a "mystery man" stood silently behind Nadia as she did her best to answer questions in the noisy, chaotic room. I would later learn he was Constantin Panait, another expatriate from Romania. Panait certainly deserves credit for having orchestrated Nadia's escape, but he subsequently kept her isolated while trying, unsuccessfully, to exploit her stardom in the United States.

"I want to have a free life," Nadia told everyone.

Her countrymen had always assumed that she had been richly rewarded by the government, but that was not the case. She had been put to pasture and assigned a job as a minor functionary in the Romanian Gymnastics Federation. By appearances, she lived in a nice house in a nice section of Bucharest with her mother and her brother. In reality, they were broke—her stipend was the equivalent of one hundred dollars a month. They spent most of their time in the kitchen because it was all they could afford to heat. They even slept in the kitchen on cold nights.

My friendship with Nadia began years after that historic moment during the 1976 Games when she scored the first perfect "10" in Olympic competition. Winding up a spectacular routine on the uneven parallel bars, Nadia dismounted with a handstand on the upper bar, from which she dropped to and flipped around the lower bar, then flew off that, swan diving into the air and ultimately landing on her feet, "sticking it." There was a delay while waiting for her marks to appear. Everyone, including commentators Cathy Rigby and Chris Schenkel, suspected some sort of controversy, perhaps a penalty. But there was no controversy, just a scoreboard inadequacy. It wasn't even possible to post the number ten on the electronic scoreboard. The officials had to settle on putting up a 1.0 to register the accomplishment.

Nadia's individual performances at the '76 Games completely overshadowed the Team gold won by the older, more experienced Soviet team. But this wasn't what made Nadia the world's greatest athlete in my mind. It was what she accomplished during the years that followed that put her in a class by herself.

When Nadia returned to her homeland in 1976 a national hero, her life changed. The Romanian Gymnastics Federation, which was basically an arm of the communist government, separated her from her coach, Bela Karolyi, and Nadia moved to Bucharest to attend college. She was suddenly on her own for the first time in her life. The result? Adolescence hit her like a bombshell. Her physical development had not progressed like that of a normal kid. My associates and I used to have discussions about why these young athletes were so thin, with not an ounce of baby fat on their tiny, sleek bodies. I confess we thought they were given drugs to retard development in order for them to continue competing with no changes in their weight or bodies. We were especially concerned at the 1979 World Championships in Fort Worth, where the Romanian squad looked especially gaunt. Nadia later explained that they had been training in Mexico and all got Montezuma's revenge! She also said that, in general, their taut, ingénue bodies were the result of intense training and a strict diet at a special school for promising gymnasts. Since the age of six, she had trained for five to six hours a day. Now on her own and going through puberty, Nadia became a typical teenager who made up for years of deprivation. No more rigorous training. Her priorities were about going to discos and eating whatever she wanted, especially ice cream.

Two years later, I was in Strasbourg, France, to produce the World Championships, where Kurt Thomas became the first American male to win the All-Around…and Nadia Comaneci completely embarrassed herself. She was overweight, out of shape, and had a new body to contend with that had womanly curves and a different center of gravity. The federation had given her only five weeks to prepare for competition. That wasn't enough time.

Anyone who had seen Nadia in Montreal was saddened. She tried but was obviously in no shape to compete. The elfin girl who charmed the entire world with a simple flick of her wrist at the end of her floor exercise in '76 had lost her magic. She even fell off the parallel bars. She did win the balance beam, but in a sea of controversy. To all observers, the medal was sort of a consolation prize based on her past record. The Romanian officials obviously agreed because Nadia didn't show for her scheduled interview with us. Instead, we watched as she and Bela dodged our cameras and ran for the exit doors of the arena.

When she returned to Romania, the little girl who always pursued excellence, who expected to be the best and win, went to work. One year later, she arrived in Tokyo for The World Cup of Gymnastics. She stepped off the plane a new woman. In all my years of hanging around world-class athletes, I have never seen a more well-toned, well-trained, and well-prepared athlete anywhere in any sport than I did that day in Tokyo. Nadia took on the world's best gymnasts from all countries, including the powerhouse teams from the Soviet Union, East Germany, and the United States. She buried them all, winning every event. Oh, she lost the balance beam in the all-around competition the first week, but only after receiving the winning marks—which were disqualified because her routine ran 1.5 seconds too long. The following week, she won all four apparatuses in the individual events. To me, this accomplishment is what made Nadia the greatest.

During the Tokyo event, I had my first run-in with the Romanian Gymnastics Federation. At ABC, we never paid for interviews. Never. In making an appointment to interview Nadia, it became obvious that something unusual was in the mix. The federation was not going to let Nadia and Bela talk on camera with our commentators Bill Flemming or Cathy Rigby unless we paid a fee. I called Jim Spence, vice president of administration in New York, to ask for guidance. Ultimately, we didn't pay any money directly, but we did arrange for gymnastics equipment to be delivered to Romania as a "thank you."

Another incident unfolded in 1977 at the Champions All meet in London during an interview Jim McKay conducted with Nadia. Nadia clearly understood English at the time (a fact she later confirmed). She chuckled when Jim mentioned rumors of her having gained fifteen kilos and often answered questions in Romanian to her interpreter before hearing a translation. A few times, Nadia started to respond directly to Jim, then caught herself and deferred to the interpreter. Years later, Nadia told us that she and her teammates were instructed to never directly answer foreigners; the official interpreter was to do that. The most telling part of their exchange was when Jim remarked that the one thing that hadn't changed since Montreal was that Nadia was still "very quiet." "Are you a shy person?" he asked. Nadia seemed reluctant to answer. She looked to the interpreter, who said to her in Romanian, "You speak too quiet. Speak louder." Nadia didn't say a word, looked around, bit her lip, then looked right at Jim. "Apparently the answer is yes," Jim said with a laugh. Nadia smiled with him, then bit her lip again and looked rather frustrated. When Jim learned that the interpreter did her own thing at times during the interview, he was furious. Obviously, it never occurred to the Romanian Gymnastics Federation that someone in our audience of millions would understand their language!

I got to know Nadia on a personal level in Bucharest in 1983 because that was the first opportunity I had to get near her. Prior to that time, Bela, through an English-speaking official, was always the go-between. Despite his lack of fluent English, he always seemed to be in charge. Turns out it was actually the government official on the scene who held the decision-making power. I later learned from Nadia that she understood English better than Bela but was forbidden to speak it. This explained why the young Romanian always seemed aloof and distant, with a mysterious quality about her, yet also seemed alert, taking everything in.

We were in Bucharest because ABC Sports bought the rights for what was to be Nadia's final public performance. A national celebration was set to take place in Sala Polivalenta, the Madison Square Garden of Bucharest. IOC President Juan Antonio Samaranch would also be on hand to bestow upon Nadia the IOC's highest honor, the Olympic Order. Nicolae Ceaușescu and thousands were in attendance. I noticed in Bucharest that Nadia's presence had completely changed. The aloofness had disappeared. She was warm and friendly and seemed eager to be with us and create a good program. We taped her coaching young gymnasts, then visited her home. As she walked us up the path to her house, I observed that the picket fence that bordered the sidewalk had been freshly painted, presumably for our American TV cameras. Years later, Nadia told me the Romanian government had also paved over the dirt road in front of her house and planted trees, shrubs, and flowers shortly before our arrival.

When we reached the top step of the front porch, Nadia opened the door of the small vestibule, where a full-sized teddy bear welcomed us. Nadia's mother and brother greeted us inside. There were two rooms on either side of the hallway. They invited us into the room on the right. What a sight it was. Hundreds of dolls and teddy bears given to Nadia by adoring fans lined the shelves and tables. Each memento was meticulously cared for. It seemed as though they were a happy diversion from the harsh realities of the life she now led in a thankless government job at minimum wage.

We crossed the hall to the room on the left. Nadia kept her medals in there, and much to my surprise, they were laid haphazardly in a drawer. Although she certainly took pride in her accomplishments and capabilities, the medals didn't seem to be as important to her as the doll collection.

I wanted to record as much footage as possible about Nadia's everyday circumstances in addition to the award presentation. Doing so would introduce the American audience to a more fun-loving Nadia, a personable young woman. I looked for an opportunity to tape a private conversation between Nadia and one of our ABC commentators, fellow Montreal Olympian Kurt Thomas. Nadia and Kurt were friends and admired each other. I thought Nadia might open up about her life a little to Kurt, now that she was no longer competing. We ended up arranging a walk for the two through a lovely public park. Our government-assigned "guide," who had stuck to us like flypaper from the moment we arrived, tagged along, of course. He was tall and intellectual-looking, right out of central casting, with his gaunt face and steel-rimmed glasses, just like the creepy Bolshevik in *Doctor Zhivago*. I was sure he was a member of Ceaușescu's Securitate, the Romanian KGB.

I walked with Kurt and Nadia as they strolled along a path for a short distance, then quietly directed the cameraman and soundman to keep going. I then sat with Mr. Securitate and a couple of officials while Kurt and Nadia walked beyond hearing range. The idea was to get Mr. Securitate to think we were just shooting B-roll footage, i.e., scenic shots for editing. Kurt and Nadia walked and talked for about ten minutes before returning.

Mission accomplished, though I would later learn that Nadia didn't say much. She was like so many other star athletes from behind the Iron Curtain—their lives were so controlled and they were so closely watched that they were cautious about saying anything that might get them into trouble.

That night, Kurt wanted to spend some time with Nadia and her family, and the rest of us wanted to go out on the town. The challenge was how to ditch our unwanted chaperone. Around nine o'clock, we told Mr. Securitate that we were going to bed and would see him the following day. He finally left the hotel…and so did we, out into the dimly lit streets of Bucharest where old ladies sheathed in babushkas swept the sidewalks with brooms made of twigs. The next morning, we all met in the lobby as scheduled.

"You had a good time at the nightclub last night?" Mr. Securitate asked as he greeted us. "But Kurt wasn't with you. Where was he?"

Wow! Welcome to life behind the Iron Curtain and international intrigue!

I was concerned there would be serious consequences for Nadia if they learned that Kurt had visited her without permission. I told Mr. Securitate that Kurt hadn't felt well and went to bed instead of going out with us. Whether he believed me or not, I have no idea, but there were no negative consequences for Nadia…as far as I know!

We spent that day at the arena preparing for the event and worked closely with a man from the local TV station who wanted to help in any way possible. Later that evening while our ABC group dined in a private room at the hotel, our Romanian colleague suddenly appeared in the doorway. He had a serious look on his face. He walked over and squatted next to me so I could lean down to hear what he had to say. He was most apologetic and seemed a little embarrassed. He told me that I would not be allowed to leave the country until the government had screened all our videotapes. This was an absolutely unacceptable request, but I told our Romanian colleague I understood and we would discuss it the following day.

After dinner, I took our associate director Kim Belton aside. Kim was an outstanding athlete himself, a six-feet-four-inch student/scholar basketball star at Stanford who played for the Phoenix Suns until a knee injury took him out of the game. I asked Kim to get all the tapes and hide them under his bed overnight while I tried to figure out what to do. Midway through a sleepless night, I got an idea.

At our breakfast meeting the next morning, I asked Kurt and Chris Schenkel to prepare two scene sets. In the first, they would introduce the event as we normally do, telling where we were and why; the second version would be a little different. We were setting up the opening shot outside the venue when Mr. Securitate arrived. He sidled up to me as if we were two spies rendezvousing in a crowded square, his eyes avoiding contact with mine.

"What about those tapes?" he uttered out of the corner of his mouth.

I explained to him that this sort of request would never be made in the United States, that we had freedom of the press. Nonetheless, I was aware that I was a guest in his country and would respect his wishes. I also told him that we would be preparing two scene sets: one to explain the excitement of this event honoring Nadia and a second to do the same, but in this version we would tell our ten to fifteen million viewers at home in America that the Romanian government had confiscated our tapes and refused to let us leave the country until they had approved the content.

Mr. Securitate looked concerned. He excused himself. When he returned in a few minutes, he told me they would no longer need to screen the tapes.

On our way to the airport, and finally rid of our official escorts, we made a little detour at our Romanian colleague's invitation. He met us at a restaurant and then led us to the TV station, where he screened archival video of Nadia. In one segment, Nadia was a pigtailed child at her gymnastics school, practicing and clowning around with her teammates during a pillow fight in the dorm. Our friend handed me a copy of the tape. This never-before-seen footage of the Olympic champion ultimately capped our *Wide World* telecast.

I saw Nadia the following year at the 1984 Los Angeles Olympic Games, which were boycotted by the Eastern Bloc countries. This was done in retaliation for the American-led boycott of the 1980 Summer Games in Moscow protesting the Soviet Union's invasion of Afghanistan. Though a strong Soviet ally, Romania still showed up in Los Angeles. I recognized the lead official from the Romanian Gymnastics Federation, Maria Login, as she was ever-present during our visit to Bucharest. Eager to overcome any ill will I had caused during that sojourn, I invited Ms. Login and other officials to a private screening of the *Wide World* program that resulted from our visit to Bucharest. Early one morning we gathered in Roone Arledge's office at our Olympic TV headquarters at ABC Television Center West. When the show concluded, I was expecting accolades for having produced a show that presented both Nadia and Romania in a fair, good light. Instead, our guests huddled together for a brief confab. Login then turned to me and asked where I got the footage of Nadia as a child. I wasn't sure whether this was the first time they were seeing the footage themselves or if they were not happy about it having aired on American television…at no cost! I knew I had to say something in response, so I told them we had seen the footage at the television station in Bucharest before we left Romania…and I didn't mention any names.

After the fall of Communism in Romania in1989, Nadia was afraid the Romanian people would resent her run to freedom. When she returned home in 1996 to marry American gymnast Bart Conner, tens of thousands of people lined the streets to cheer as she and Bart made their way to the cathedral. I remember taking home video of the couple as they exited the church and thinking I had just witnessed another perfect "10" in Nadia's life—the end of a Cinderella story in which the heroine rescues herself *and* gets the handsome prince.

4

Leading Ladies

In 1967, Roone gave me my first opportunity to direct figure skating. The event was the US National Figure Skating Championships in Omaha, Nebraska. I tried a few new things: a low camera cut through the hockey boards at center ice and a feature about school figures with a camera looking directly down from rafters above while Peggy Fleming, the National ladies champion, traced circular patterns below.

I was quite anxious as the coverage began. Roone always felt that people used the word "anxious" when they really meant "eager," but there was no doubt in this case. I was just a neophyte with no sensitivity to the emotional quality of a skater's program, to the ebb and flow of the movements up and down the ice, or to the rhythm of the camera work flowing with the music. All that mattered was that my crew and I caught the skaters on camera and in the frame.

About a week after Nationals, I was in Grenoble, France, preparing for the upcoming Winter Olympics. In the car with Jim on our way to dinner, Roone brought up my rather embarrassing directorial debut in figure skating. He was gently, but clearly, critical of it. He talked to me about a sports television director's need to have a sixth sense. He said that sports action was not predictable, and great directors must be able to anticipate movement and action as it develops in front of the cameras. He said that some are born with this gift, and some acquire it with experience. The conversation ended without Roone firing me. I was relieved—and assumed that meant he would give me a chance to gain that experience.

Although I spent the next few years in the producer role and directed only occasionally, I was grateful for Roone's Grenoble pep talk when, despite hardly being able to skate, I was inducted into the US Figure Skating Hall of Fame in 2003 for my contributions to the sport. My journey to directing competence consisted of on-the-job training combined with drawing upon experiences working on television dramas earlier in my career. These programs were shot on one-stage studios and were methodically preplanned. With homemade models and a set of floor plans, like most directors, I prepared by blocking the actors and the traffic of two boom microphones and three cameras. It was like playing Tetris. Next, I created shot lists for each cameraman. Zoomar lenses were not yet widely in use, so each camera had a turret with three lenses of different lengths screwed into it. I had to determine not only the sequence of shots but also which lenses the cameramen were to swivel into place for each shot and from what position on the studio floor. It was all very technical.

With skating, my studio was an ice arena, more than twenty times the size. Instead of three cameras, I had at least seven. Instead of relatively static actors moving within a confined space according to script, there were one or two skaters moving at high speed. And although each routine was preset, that didn't mean the skater couldn't deviate or slip, and then there was all the action during warm-up sessions and off the ice, which was completely unpredictable.

Like directing, skating has its technical side, upon which the fundamentals are based. More important, however, is the artistic side. If both the skater and I were doing our jobs well, the viewers weren't distracted by the technical aspects of either the skating or the camera work. Seamless, flowing skating was our objective. Prior to the Calgary Winter Olympics in 1988, William Taaffe interviewed me for *Sports Illustrated*. Taaffe wrote that "in no other sport was there a closer affinity between a TV director and the sport's participants than figure skating." He described the director as the TV choreographer. As I explained to Taaffe, I approached skating as the ultimate fusion of entertainment and sport. He added it was also the ultimate marriage between sport and the tube.

My drama skills also proved to be useful. I learned to get inside the competitors the same way I would a character. For many of the performances I was going to cover, I spent hours at the rink studying each skater's program and taking notes until I could emotionally glide along with each stroke, feel every movement, and know the climactic moments. Then I would try to marry them all with the camera work. If I cut late in the middle of a jump, caught the skater's backside on the landing, or missed her smiling face, I had failed us both—which happened more times than I'd like to admit. Let's just say I grew to understand why professional golfers often miss what *seem* to be easy putts!

There was one more life experience that surprisingly turned out to be perfect training for a television director, and that was my love for radio as a child. In the 1940s, radio was the center of home entertainment. I loved listening to soap operas, and *Grand Central Station* was one of my favorites. It opened with the blaring whistle of a locomotive and the voice of a man: "…Drawn by the magnetic force of the fantastic metropolis, day and night…great trains rush toward the Hudson River…" His cadence and volume surged along with the chugging engines and grinding of metal wheels against track. "…And dive with a roar…[into] Grand Central Station!…crossroads of a million private lives, a gigantic stage on which are played a thousand dramas daily!"

By the time I heard that final line, my heart was racing like a runaway train.

When you watch television, you merely watch. When you listened to radio drama, you actually participated in the production because you used your mind to "see" the scenes. My radio addiction expanded my imagination and taught me to visualize things and recognize a good story. A good story meant good entertainment, and that was our ultimate goal.

So with a pinch of theater, a dash of radio, a little ingenuity, and a marvelous technical crew, I learned to place and use television cameras so that they wouldn't merely document a skater's program, as they did in Omaha, but enhance it, help tell the skater's story. And there were so many good stories to tell during the years I directed skating coverage for ABC…especially when it came to the women.

Here's to the ladies who skate…

PEGGY

I have seen thousands of skating performances over the course of my career, and I am often asked which one is the most memorable. Many come to mind. Who could forget Jayne Torvill and Christopher Dean's "Bolero" for Ice Dance Olympic gold in 1984? Their pas de deux was so erotic we all felt like voyeurs watching them. In 1986 at the Twenty-Fifth Anniversary of US Figure Skating's Memorial Fund, the usually light and entertaining Scott Hamilton turned solemn with his sermon on ice to "Battle Hymn of the Republic." The Olympic champion's stunning tribute to the members of the 1961 US World Team, who were all killed in a plane crash on their way to the World Championships, didn't leave a dry eye in the house. Then there was the awe and inspiration of '88 gold medalist Brian Boitano when he skated on a frozen lake deep in the Alaskan wilderness. And I can still feel the intense emotion and drama of Chinese pair Xue Shen and Hongbo Zhao skating to Puccini's *Turandot* for their second World title in 2003. Their program was so ardently expressive, the American audience began its standing ovation thirty seconds before the final pose.

These were all spine-tingling performances, but the one that rises above them all took place in a cold, empty arena in Lake Placid in the fall of 1979, a few months before the XIII Olympic Winter Games. We had just finished taping an ice-skating competition in the brand-new Lake Placid Olympic Center. Though the town had cleared out, the ABC crew remained to await the arrival of the 1968 Olympic gold medalist, Peggy Fleming. A few months prior, Dick Button, the 1948 and 1952 Olympic men's champion who became our expert analyst, mentioned that Peggy was skating better than ever in Ice Capades, a popular traveling ice show at the time. Roone suggested that we feature Peggy in some way in our presentation of the 1980 Games.

I was a bit keyed up about working with Peggy. For one, I did not know her well. I served as an AD during the '68 Games, which meant I spent most of my time in the tape room in the broadcast center. I had also heard that Peggy had been given the impression by people who wanted her to skate on another network that ABC didn't like her. Hard to think that someone who was the pride of the skating world and a national treasure would believe this, but that was part of Peggy's appeal—her unassuming nature, despite her stardom. I was also a little worried because earlier that year I had produced the telecast of a North American skating competition in San Jose, California, Peggy's hometown. Peggy was in attendance, so we requested an interview, to which she somewhat hesitantly agreed. She was certainly gracious and conversant during her on-air chat, but as I watched on the monitor inside the mobile van outside the arena, I sensed some reservation on her part.

All this was on my mind while I waited for her in Lake Placid, not to mention the fact that we hadn't really planned what we were going to tape. Then came the knock on the door, and there she was…smiling, friendly, and absolutely beautiful. I know now that she was as anxious about meeting the crew and me as we were about meeting her. To start things off on the right skate, we screened her 1968 Olympic performance. When the reel stopped, she turned to us and said, "Thank you. I've never seen that before." Quite amazing that she had never seen her free skate in full, but back then, even Olympic champions didn't have home recording devices like VCRs and DVRs or the instant access to film and video history that we enjoy today on YouTube.

The next morning, the Olympic Arena awaited us for what turned out to be a fifteen-hour day. We began by transforming what was a scene of competition into a theatrical space. Once again, the cameramen dragged the heavy cables across the seats and aisles to new camera positions and lugged seven huge cameras into place. Eight giant spotlights were schlepped to the upper level. Then we faced the challenge of blacking out the arena, which was a modern structure with great expanses of glass. That accomplished, we hung a huge curtain of black velour, eight feet high and 596 feet long, around the perimeter of the ice surface. Done. We had achieved our desired effect: a black void in which a glowing skater would look like she was gliding through the cosmos.

Peggy arrived at nine that morning with her choreographer, 1960 Olympic Pair Champion Bob Paul. The three of us kept out of the way of the hustling crew as we discussed the three numbers we would try to get on tape before day's end. A few hours later, we were ready to do a complete run-through. Peggy changed into her costume, the follow-spot operators fired up their arc lights, the cameramen settled into their positions, and I went to the truck to watch on the monitors.

When all was finally ready for the first number, the arena went silent and dark, except for a pool of warm light at center ice. As the first gentle piano notes of "Song for Cynthia" began, Peggy glided into the light in an elegant white gown, the skirt made of narrow white ribbons designed to ripple in the breeze. She was no longer the shy, young woman in the simple, chartreuse dress she made famous while skating for Olympic gold in Grenoble. She was a prima ballerina, skating with the maturity and grace of a Margot Fonteyn on ice.

I was mesmerized by seven moving images on the monitors before me. She was magical from every angle. There were no triples, no gymnastics, no double combinations—just gorgeous, flowing movement. Her spread eagle looked more like a wafting swan, and the entire program had the essence of the night flight of a white bird in a full moon's glow. After a climactic spin, the music began to fade, and Peggy lowered herself onto one knee, her left leg stretching behind her. Her right arm rose upward, as if reaching for a star. She held the pose—it seemed that star would not let go.

No one moved.

Then the clap of a pair of hands severed the silence…then another… then another. I watched as seven jaded, burly, "I've-seen-it-all" *Monday Night Football* cameramen stepped from behind their cameras, applauding. The spot operators then joined the tribute, followed by the stagehands.

I had never seen anything like it and haven't since.

We had all been working in that colossal ice bucket for four straight days. We were freezing and exhausted. There was no magnificent mountain providing a breathtaking backdrop, no orchestra playing an electrifying symphony, no gold medal at stake creating tension, and no spectators sitting in the 7,700 seats, charging the air with electricity. And yet, Peggy Fleming managed to turn that massive void into a grand cathedral and fill it with the heat and energy of a gospel choir. We had not just watched a typical go-through-the-motions run-through; we had witnessed a performance—the *first* Miracle on Ice that would occur in the Lake Placid Olympic Ice Arena.

Peggy's performance was further heightened by a new point of view. For years I had struggled to find a way to bring the viewer onto the ice with the skater, which meant having a camera that moved with the motion as opposed to pivoting on a stationary base or zooming in or out. In early sports television, that's pretty much all cameras did. The picture on screen was basically the fan's view from the bleachers. I had fiddled with all kinds of contraptions: wagons, hand-pushed ice makers—none worked. I consulted with a cameraman named Ned Dowd who had filmed some ice action for the 1977 feature film *Slap Shot*. He told me he put a camera on a shovel and, because he was a hockey player himself, was able to skillfully slide the shovel across the ice while the camera hitched to it caught the skating action. That solution might have been good for low-level blade/puck/stick action in a motion picture situation, but it would have limited use for figure skating. Steadicams hadn't been invented yet, either—television cameras were large and unwieldy. Ned then suggested we try a wheelchair. It would be free to roll and slide alongside the skater—as long as there were no cables attached. To resolve this challenge, I worked with some of the guys in engineering who built a wooden platform into the chair. This way, all the equipment needed was contained in the chair: the cameraman, the videotape recorder housed within the platform, and the wires connecting them all.

From rink side, the awkward pas de trois among Peggy and her two skating partners—a brawny hockey player pushing a wheelchair and Bill Sullivan sitting in that chair with a forty-pound camera on his shoulder—looked rather comical. But on our monitors, and later on television, we were all, for the first time, transported right alongside the balletic Olympic champion.

We shot three numbers that day in Lake Placid. "Song for Cynthia" aired during a pre-Olympic prime-time special. A disco number that Jim dubbed "Lady in Red" because it was hot and jazzy (not the sort of thing Peggy was known for) was scheduled to air early during our telecast of the ladies' long program competition on Saturday night—always the climactic event of our Winter Olympic broadcasts. The third number, "Some Enchanted Evening," was intended to air the night before the ladies' final to promote it. Expecting the result of a certain hockey game on that Friday to be determined very early in the contest, Roone planned to cut away to "Some Enchanted Evening" when the hockey score became a runaway.

As Robert Burns wrote, "The best laid schemes o' mice an' men / Gang aft agley." By the third period, the US Olympic Hockey Team, made up of amateur and college players, was leading the mighty Soviet Team in what is considered to be the greatest upset in the history of sport. I stood in the control room of the broadcast center cheering with everyone else, but with mixed emotions. As the minutes ticked away toward the glorious, unbelievable conclusion, I knew that the ice holding "Some Enchanted Evening" over the cutting room floor was getting thinner and thinner. When Al Michaels shouted, "Do you believe in miracles?...*Yes!*" I agreed, but I was not happy that America would never see Peggy skate to the *South Pacific* ballad.

The next morning, Roone hummed the melody as he passed me in the hall of the broadcast center. Rascal. What I didn't know at that moment was that a blessing in disguise was in the works. Roone had decided to air both numbers that night, and Jim would interview Peggy between the two performances. That telecast turned out to be the highest-rated night in Olympic television history at the time. About seventy-six million people saw the "new" Peggy, significantly more than in 1968. Her career was revitalized, and Roone hired her as an expert commentator, something she still does today.

About a year later, I returned from an overseas assignment to find a package waiting for me in my office. It contained a beautiful wooden plaque, upon which were mounted two skate blades. The inscription began,

> On a long, long day in September 1979 at the
> new Olympic Field House, you and I worked
> out the television arrangements of "Some
> Enchanted Evening," "Song for Cynthia," and
> "Disco." These blades were there…

I would throw all my Emmys into the Hudson River to keep this one memento.

TRIXI AND JANET

Dick Button burst through the door of the producer's suite, breathless and excited.

"I just witnessed something I've never seen in all my years in figure skating!"

We were about a half hour into our production meeting for the 1971 World Figure Skating Championships in Lyon, France, and Dick was late.

"There was actually an audience for compulsory figures!" he went on. "Not only that, but when the third figure was completed, everyone jumped over the hockey boards and went to look at Trixi's tracings!"

Beatrix "Trixi" Schuba was a figure-skating wizard. She won the World title that year and continued her reign in 1972 at the Sapporo Olympics and World Championships in Calgary. Sadly, nobody cared.

No one cared because daring double axles, sizzling sit spins, and stunning spirals were not in this Austrian's bag of tricks. Trixi's forte was compulsory figures, "school figures" as they were commonly called, and she did them better than anyone…ever. For most people, watching compulsories was a little like watching water freeze. Only the skating elite could truly appreciate the skills involved. And yet, to watch a human body balance atop a double-edged blade and methodically stop and start and swirl as she transferred energy from one edge to the other while carving perfect circles in patterns on the ice, and then do it again on the weaker foot, was truly amazing.

As unpopular as they were, the school figures accounted for half of a skater's total score. There were forty-one figures in the International Skating Union rulebook. Six were chosen each season, and three were announced just before a competition began. After tracing the first pattern, the skater went over the same micro-thin groove two more times, ideally leaving only one track in the ice upon completion. It was an exercise in striving for perfection. For the competitors, who had spent thousands of predawn hours practicing in arctic-like ice rinks, this part of the competition was nerve-racking. The slightest loss of balance or inertia could cost a medal.

But for anyone watching, it was frosty boresville. Skating fans saw virtually none of this part of the competition. They wanted to see, and we devoted our telecasts to, the free skate. There were, in fact, many people who resented that Trixi Schuba was the World Figure Skating Champion. They felt that arithmetic made her champion, not skating. To top it off, Trixi didn't have that "it girl" appeal like her predecessors, Carol Heiss, the 1960 Olympic champion, and Peggy Fleming. The finicky fans just weren't eager to see a tall, big-boned Austrian with a dowdy hairdo skate. Trixi was too serious, almost dour. Her strokes were strong and determined, businesslike, not balletic and flowing. For audiences who came to be entertained, they felt little connection with Trixi. Worst of all, Trixi was constantly contrasted with her rival, American Janet Lynn. Trixi's free skating paled in comparison to Janet's wondrous artistry and joy on the ice. To compound matters, Janet was adorable. Her Midwestern charm, petite blonde good looks, and sunshine smile captured the hearts of fans everywhere. Janet was held back, however, by her poor school figures and slips or falls in key competitions. I also think she was too good-natured, too "nice." She didn't possess that killer instinct I'd seen in other skaters.

Carol Heiss once told me that it's much more difficult for a woman to compete in figure skating than it is for a man. A man can be in harmony with his competitive nature, his masculinity. He can appear aggressive and powerful in the attack; whereas a woman is expected to be the ballerina—graceful, feminine, and flowing. But she must simultaneously harbor the same aggressiveness—that drive to dominate the battle—beneath her graceful athleticism.

Trixi and Janet perfectly represented both truths in this paradox, as exemplified by the awards ceremony in Lyon in 1971. Trixi stood on the top podium with a gold medal around her neck and waving a bouquet of flowers while the crowd chanted, "Janet, Janet, Janet!" The roar was so thunderous that the eighteen-year-old American, who finished fourth, was nudged back to the rink side to take a bow.

A year later in Canada, Trixi defended her World title, and Janet moved up to third. The traditional Sunday afternoon exhibition rolled around and, usually, the Ladies Champion was the most anticipated and final skater of the show. But Trixi's lack of charisma and free skating appeal didn't warrant placing her last in the show, notwithstanding her two World titles and recent Olympic gold. The organizers gave her the faint prestige of ending the first act, which got her out of the way early to set the stage for the real draws: American John Misha Petkevich, Soviet pair skaters Irina Rodnina and Alexei Ulanov, and Soviet ice dancers Lyudmila Pakhomova and Alexander Gorshkov, and, of course, Janet Lynn.

I'm ashamed to admit that our production crew felt the same way about Trixi. As sports journalists, protocol demanded that we show the winner, but as producers of television entertainment, we wished we didn't have to. We had also received letters from outraged viewers who objected to our taking precious airtime for Trixi's "pedestrian performances." I was especially torn on a personal level because earlier in the week, we interviewed Trixi regarding the International Skating Union's impending rule change. The short program was going to be added to the competition, which meant that the value of the compulsory figures would be reduced from 50 percent to 40. With the short program garnering 20 percent and the long program 40 percent, free skating would now own the majority of the final score. In other words, the ISU had made it clear that school figures would never dominate the result of a competition again (in 1990, they were eliminated from the sport altogether). Future competitions would favor skaters like Janet. One could say that this rule change was a backhanded tribute to Trixi's unparalleled skills and dominance in the art of school figures.

I had never actually met Trixi, despite having televised her performances for a number of years. Based upon the impression she gave on the ice, I expected to meet a sullen, possibly unpleasant person. Was I wrong! Beatrix Schuba was not only gracious and accommodating to our broadcasting demands, she was funny, warmly gregarious, genuine, attractive, and lovable! Under that unflattering haircut and bland costume was a wonderful woman.

Days later, seated in the producer's chair in the TV mobile van, I was a bit blue as Trixi was announced for her exhibition performance. Usually skaters experience a moment in the sun during exhibitions, a time to skate free of the pressure of competition and only for the fans' adulation. I feared for Trixi as her music began, then heard Joe Aceti, our associate director at the time, on the headset.

"You know what she ought to do. She ought to do a school figure."

The goose bumps started at my toes and shot right to the top of my balding pate. Of course! I relayed the brilliant idea over the private line to the announcers.

"Dick, when she comes off the ice, tell her to go back out and do a school figure."

With all the noise of the music, he wasn't sure what he had heard. "Really?"

"Yes!" I said louder. "Tell her to go out and do a school figure!"

Trixi had not skated well, even for her. She was also jarred from a fall and out of breath. Applause was respectful, but brief. Dick took her arm and dropped the microphone out of range. She looked quizzical and suspect as he spoke—she was wise enough to know that an encore was not called for. The applause had long since died out. Nevertheless, Trixi stroked her way back to center ice.

The music playback man at rink side had no idea what was going on. Completely confused, he started another piece of music he had on hand for Trixi. Baffled herself, Trixi started skating another program! Meanwhile back in the truck, I took a deep breath and said a prayer for Trixi, but I was determined that in this, her last appearance as an amateur, she simply had to do her thing. I toggled the communication switch.

"Dick! When she comes off, tell her again! Tell her to go out and do a school figure!"

Trixi finished her unwelcomed encore. The crowd hardly applauded. She skated to the barrier, and, once again, Dick urged her to go out and trace a figure. When she reluctantly returned to center ice, the audience was stunned. What a display of unfounded ego! I heard a "boo" and a derisive whistle.

The music tech raised his arms in frustration. Luckily, he had no more music to play. Trixi took the starting pose for a figure called a back paragraph loop. The crowd hushed and Trixi pushed off. Gradually, some clapping broke the silence. By the time she had completed the figure, five thousand people were on their feet screaming "bravos" above the din.

Overwhelmed by the praise and love coming from the fans, Trixi broke into a huge, heartfelt smile and bowed graciously. The applause carried her all the way off the ice and then some. It was so loud, our microphone barely heard her say, "Oh mein Got!" Back in the truck, we all felt relieved and proud as Trixi Schuba, who had never experienced the euphoria of a standing ovation in all her years of competing and winning Olympic and World titles, finally received her due. Like it or not, under the rules of the game at the time, Trixi was indomitable. She deserved each and every gold medal. She was a legitimate, and in her own way, great champion.

Trixi turned professional and signed a contract with the European-owned Holiday on Ice. They sent her to La Costa, the posh Southern California spa, to trim down and get into showbiz shape. She emerged from her extreme makeover practically unrecognizable. In a Vegas-showgirl-like costume, she provocatively skated a program with sexy music and choreography…and it began and ended with a school figure.

Meanwhile, Janet, with two roadblocks out of her way—Trixi and a diminished factor for compulsories—headed to the 1973 World Championships in Bratislava. She skated her best figures ever to head into the short program in second place. The title finally in reach, she fell twice in the very event that would have helped her win. She slipped to twelfth. Even though she went on to win the long program, it wasn't enough. Janet Lynn, beloved everywhere she skated and considered by many to be the greatest female skater of all time, would never win an ISU World or Olympic Championship.

Disappointed, yes, but motivated by her devout Christian faith, Janet was always skating more for the sheer joy of her sport than for anything else. She has told me that she does not know why she fell on the flying sit spin, usually an easy maneuver for her. It just happened. She made a mistake. But she got up with a smile, the same way she had after her spill during the long program at the Olympics the year before.

Janet's inspired skating in Sapporo, and the way she handled misfortune, etched her spirit in the hearts of the Japanese people so deeply that twenty-four years later, the Nagano Olympic Committee invited Janet to be a goodwill ambassador for the 1998 Winter Games. During a visit to Japan prior to the Nagano Games, Janet's press junket included a stop at the apartment she inhabited during the Sapporo Olympics. The complex had been converted to private residences since then. Inside the apartment, her chaperones, who were members of the Japanese press and the Nagano Olympic Committee, proudly pointed to a certain wall in the bedroom. Though the apartment had been repainted many times, still preserved were the words Janet had written in large letters upon her departure in 1972: "Peace and Love, Janet Lynn."

Janet's hosts then took her to the Makomanai Arena, where she had competed. There wasn't any ice, but the reporters walked Janet over to a certain spot on the floor. One reporter told Janet that she was too young to have seen her skate in '72, but she knew the exact spot where Janet had taken one of her famous falls. Janet was asked to please sit down on the spot so they could take a picture of her there—still smiling.

DOROTHY

She skated onto the ice, adorably fourteen with bangs across her forehead and a pink bow in her hair. She was competing in her first World Championships. Just weeks earlier, she watched on TV as Janet Lynn was awarded the bronze in Sapporo behind Trixi and Canada's Karen Magnussen. Trixi would be turning professional after Worlds, and Janet the following year, so the curtain was starting to rise on the teenager from the Skating Club of New York…Dorothy Hamill.

Dick Button, known as the sage of the skating world by then, told us to keep an eye out for this new girl who skated with both athleticism and grace, so we made sure to tape Dorothy's program. There was definitely something about her, though I wasn't sure exactly what. Maybe it was that all-American-girl-next-door air about her, or the cute way she squinted in the "Kiss and Cry" area as she tried to decipher her marks on the distant scoreboard. Dorothy seemed a little insecure, yet once she was on the ice and the music started, she was completely in command.

Dorothy finished seventh at Worlds that year, so her admirable performance did not air on our telecast. These days, if a sporting event exceeds the allotted time slot on the network, it likely finishes up on cable. During the early decades of *Wide World*, we always wrestled with the time limitation. The way athletes got on the show was either to win or be spectacular—spectacular meaning something such as getting gored by a rodeo bull or crashing into *and* over a barrier at two hundred miles per hour. At Worlds in 1971, Dorothy may not have been spectacular, but her talent and charisma were certainly special. Two weeks later, we were able to squeeze in some of her program "joined in progress" (or "J-I-P-ed," as we used to say). Such exposure, even though just a few minutes, helped this new skater begin to forge a reputation, which is crucial in a sport that is judged.

The depth of Dorothy's competitive pride, and I would also say her character, was first demonstrated two years later at the 1974 World Championships in Munich. She arrived as the newly crowned US National Champion and entered the free skate in second place after the school figures. Our cameras followed Dorothy warming up on the ice while the previous skater, German Gerti Schanderl, awaited her marks. The technical marks appeared on the scoreboard, and the crowd started to boo and whistle. As each mark was announced over the PA system, the protest got louder and louder and escalated again when Dorothy's name was announced. The more the announcer said, the louder the disgruntled audience got, shattering Dorothy's concentration. She unraveled as she paced the ice. In the booth, Jim remarked that Gerti had put in a good performance, but it was a "bad performance on the part of the crowd, just a miserable thing for people to do to a competitor." "No, no, no," Dick disagreed. "She'll be all right. She's a very emotional girl. She's up one day and down the next."

As he said this, the announcer made another attempt to quiet the spectators and introduce Dorothy, but their derision persisted. The "temperamental girl," as Dick described her, just couldn't take it any longer. She broke into tears and retreated off the ice into the comfort of her father's arms.

"Well, I tell you something, Dick," Jim said, talking over him and the noise of the crowd, "I'd be pretty down if I were fighting for a World Championship myself, and I came out and ten thousand people booed me for five minutes!"

Dorothy couldn't comprehend at the moment that the German crowd wasn't deriding her personally; they just thought their home-town girl deserved a better score. Gerti's marks did move her into third place temporarily, but that wasn't enough as far as her countrymen were concerned.

What Dick was referring to in his commentary was that there was always "something" about Dorothy. Her school figures were good, but never the best, and rumors were circulating that she was a bit head-strong. She had a delicate mixture of determination, independence, and emotional vulnerability. Then again, she was only sixteen years old and competing on a world stage. In a pre-event interview, Dorothy's coach, Carlo Fassi, addressed that independence, or perhaps recalcitrance, on Dorothy's part. He said, in a way that only he could with his thick Italian accent, "Whata we need here is a leetle bit a East-ah Germany." He was referring, of course, to the Spartan, no-frills, obsessive dedication to training for which the East German athletes were notorious at the time.

But the young woman from Riverside, Connecticut, showed us all she didn't need such training. With our cameras still watching, officials approached her and offered her a few minutes to go backstage and regain her composure while the raucous crowd settled down. In an instant, Dorothy's whole demeanor changed. There would be no bending of the rules for her. No, sir. With shoulders back and head down and forward, she charged back onto the ice like a skating gladiator. This time, the crowd voiced its support with encouraging applause. Dorothy broke into a smile, then eased into her starting pose. Apologies made and accepted, the arena finally got quiet. From the music's opening flourish, skating greatness was in the air. Dick predicted that the "up-and-down girl" would skate the program of her life, and she did, attacking every move, driving forward to a standing ovation and second place.

Jim came to my hotel room that night and asked me not to edit out the little disagreement that he and Dick had at the beginning of Dorothy's free skate. Dick, on the other hand, kindly asked me to cut it or rerecord the commentary. We talked it over. He understood that from my point of view as a producer, there was no question—the commentary would air "as is" because it was great television.

Dorothy's silver at Worlds was the beginning of her road to Olympic gold in '76 at Innsbruck, yet once more she would skate into the fray not long after that flame extinguished. Dorothy had never won a World title, yet some advised her to turn professional right away. A loss at the World

Championships only a few weeks later would taint her Olympic victory, not to mention the value of professional contracts and endorsements. But Dorothy, though only nineteen, knew that if she didn't participate in the '76 Worlds, she would regret it later in life and would always wonder if she could have won that one elusive title. So she competed in Goteborg, Sweden, and once again defeated her rival, Dianne DeLeeuw, as she had in Innsbruck…and forever became known as World and Olympic Champion Dorothy Hamill.

As Dick said that day in Munich, "The girl is up when the pressure is on," and that virtue would carry over into her professional career while shooting her first television special for ABC. Gary Smith and Dwight Hemion, the best variety team in the business, were set to produce and direct the show. Because they were not familiar with figure skating, I was brought on as a consultant.

Musical film star Gene Kelly was the show's special guest, and "Singin' in the Rain," the song he made famous in the movie of the same name, was featured in the program. Dorothy was going to skate the part Mr. Kelly danced in the film, and he would play the cop who walks up at the end, his arms crossed in disapproval. We shot the special in Toronto at a studio equipped with ice. At one point, Mr. Kelly told Dorothy that he felt bad for her because when he danced the famous number at MGM on a sound stage, they warmed the rain water. In Dorothy's case, we couldn't warm the water or it would melt the ice! So, hour after hour, take after take, trouper Dorothy skated under an ice-cold shower—and into illness.

The following morning was overcast, dank, and bone cold as we set up outdoors and taped a segment. We did yet another that night. Dorothy spent the late afternoon resting in a hotel room across the street. Meanwhile, I ran around town buying space blankets, a Coleman heater, and extra-large sock slippers and metal hand-warming devices that I used to concoct skate warmers since they hadn't been invented yet!

Night had fallen and all was ready to go in the park. The ice was prepared, the backdrop of new and old city buildings was warmly glowing from the lighting artistry of Bill Klages, and conductor Ian Fraser and the orchestra were waiting to take their places on the ice surface. At the hotel, the makeup man made his final touches on Dorothy's clammy face, then reported to the director that his star was feverish and would never be able to perform. A budgetary disaster was at stake, and the clock was ticking.

Dorothy swallowed two of the strongest over-the-counter cold pills available in Canada, and we left the hotel. She paused in the middle of the street, right on the trolley tracks.

"I can't do it," she said. "I can't do this."

We looked at each other.

"You don't have to," I said. "You're the star. It can only be done when you're ready and able."

Suddenly, it was if I were watching that sixteen-year-old in Munich waiting for the crowd to stop booing. She straightened up with soldierly determination and turned toward the park.

"Let's go."

And the girl who initially learned to skate because her friends could skate backward and she couldn't, worked until the wee hours of the morning.

E. Z.

Elaine Zayak trained mostly in the company of boys and refused to be outdone by them. As a result, her skating was athletic and lively. She also compensated for her consistently low school figures by showing off her strength, jumping. At the US Nationals in 1980, Elaine landed *seven* triple jumps in her free skate and started the jumping craze in ladies' figure skating. At the World Championships in 1982, she landed six triples to win the title. In an effort to control the evolution of the sport, as it did in the wake of Trixi's domination in figures, the ISU quickly changed the rules to limit the number of triple (and later, quadruple) jumps in one program. It's called the "Zayak Rule."

In 1983, I visited Elaine's training rink in Monsey, New York, where she prepared for the upcoming Winter Olympics in Sarajevo. As I watched Elaine practice, I got to talking with her coach, Peter Burrows. He quietly revealed something that was not public knowledge at the time. The '82 World Champion skated with a major handicap. She had only half a left foot!

I was stunned. Of course, I believed him, but it seemed impossible! A world-class figure skater with half a foot! I couldn't help but turn my eyes toward the ice and watch Elaine skate—not only with renewed respect but to look for some indication of her disability.

Couldn't detect a thing.

Peter explained that when Elaine was two, she was running toward her father in their yard while he was driving a tractor mower. She slipped and her left foot slid into the whirring blades, severing it between the second and third toe all the way through her heel. The doctors couldn't save the foot and recommended the toddler try roller or ice skating to help her improve her balance. Her mom took her to a local rink and filled the void in her left boot with a scrunched sock. The skates felt better than her street shoes. When she stepped onto the ice, she stroked away. She was a natural.

I had been chronicling Elaine's skating career since 1979, even videotaped her roller skating on the Great Wall of China, but never saw the slightest hint that she had any unusual physical challenges. She had spent her young life hiding it. Shortly before the '84 Games, Elaine found the courage to reveal her foot in an "Up Close and Personal" profile. As she removed her sock for the TV camera, it opened our eyes to the reason she was never very good in figures. She was unable to roll her left foot.

Recently when I spoke with Elaine, she told me that her foot was also the reason she always put on her skates in a corner away from everyone and kept a towel nearby, ready to cover up in case anyone got too close. How agonizing that must have been for her at event after event. At the same time, how admirable that this extraordinary champion would then lace up, take the ice, and dazzle audiences and judges with her kinetic skating.

ROZ

I got my keenest insight into the psyche of the female competitor during a ladies practice session at the 1984 Nationals in Salt Lake City. For that, I thank Rosalynn Sumners, the defending World and National Champion and favorite for the '84 Winter Games in Sarajevo. Until that day, I had always assumed that skaters showed up for practice simply to focus on their training. But there is another motive…a higher goal. And that is to stand out—to make an impression so brazen that the other skaters in your session merely bleach into the dullness of the scratched-up ice because all eyes in the arena are only on you.

These practice sessions are sparsely attended, but diehard skating fans buy tickets to watch these moments of preparation, and the media is often present. More important, however, the judges come to familiarize themselves with the programs, and the skaters aim to impress them. This is when the competition really begins. Each of the four or five skaters on the ice wants to be noticed and studied above all others. And the female skaters, like their sisters in other walks of life, whether actresses, politicians, or friends headed out for a night on the town, know that great hair, sublime shoes, or a fabulous outfit are going to turn heads.

I was about to learn that Rosalynn Sumners was a mistress of magnetism.

I was at my usual spot at rink side, planning camera blocking with an associate when a flash of color caught my attention. Sailing across the ice came a blonde goddess in a lavender bodysuit that clung deliciously to her womanly curves. She sensationally accessorized with matching boot covers and gloves that extended her bodylines to beguiling extremes.

To watch Roz skate…well…no woman ever emitted more sensuality on the ice. How the ice did not melt was beyond me. When Roz finished her session, I couldn't help my caveman self. I told her that her outfit was the sexiest thing I'd ever seen. She smiled contentedly. I would later learn why—she had the ensemble created exclusively for the practice sessions during Olympic year, and it certainly did its job. I don't remember any other skaters in the session.

Peggy Fleming, who was commentating that week, also explained to me that although a female skater, of course, wants to be the best technically and the most graceful, she also wants to be the center of attention. The same goes for the competition warm-up periods, which are filled with high tension. The top skaters actually have a set routine that is pre-planned with their coaches. Sometimes intimidation is part of the strategy, where one skater gets a little too close to another, preventing the

execution of a jump or just "getting in their space." But the most important thing is to be noticed. Although performance is paramount, being
attractive also helps, especially in a sport that is judged—and especially
if you are female.

Roz and I kidded each other about the outfit for years. Sometime
after she turned professional, a soft, puffy manila envelope arrived in
the mail. Inside, I found the lavender body suit. I think it belongs in the
Smithsonian.

KAT

Roz narrowly lost the gold in '84 to the ravishing Katarina Witt of the
German Democratic Republic. Katarina was a highly disciplined competitor who skated to win and did so with a confident smile on her face.
She was also rather distant, a characteristic typical of most athletes from
behind the Iron Curtain—and for good reason. Sports programs were run
by the governments, and athletes were instructed not to fraternize in any
way. The East Germans seemed to take their sports even more seriously
than the Soviets, which may explain why Katarina was always shielded
by government officials and her rigid coach, Jutta Müller, who protected
her like a lioness. I remember at Calgary wanting to tell Katarina to look
straight into the center camera in her final pose for the long program,
but I couldn't speak to her directly. I had to go through Müller, who all
but blew me off. I doubt she passed on my request because Katarina
looked at the judges. Gold medal won, but golden opportunity to make
people around the world feel like she was looking directly at them—gone.
Forever.

Four years later, after the 1988 Olympics in Calgary, the men's gold
medalist, Brian Boitano, invited Katarina to costar with him in a television special. Such an opportunity was unprecedented for a skater from
the Eastern Bloc. Katarina was excited about the prospect, but getting
permission from her government to perform in an American TV special

presented a major hurdle. Katarina was given an informal OK by some commissar, but it had to be officially approved. Determined to appear in the program, Katarina asked Brian and me to call her at an appointed time and day. On a very hot Labor Day with the air conditioning in the office minimized for the holiday, I was already sweating as the ABC operator placed the call. First, she picked up Brian in San Francisco, then dialed the number in East Berlin. "Allo," a male voice answered clear and strong. I assumed he was a Communist Party official. Feeling like a spy in a World War II movie, I asked to speak to Katarina Witt. Sure enough, she was there. I imagined her in a stark room, dimly lit by a single lightbulb dangling from the ceiling. Words went back and forth in both German and English. I could sense the official's resistance, but Katarina, who had some clout due to her global superstardom, persisted. In the end, she was granted permission to do the project, with Brian and me as telephonic witnesses across the Atlantic.

"Canvas of Ice," starring the two Calgary champions, was set to air in December. Before then, my crew and I headed to East Germany to shoot two numbers with Katarina. We flew into West Berlin, then headed to the Berlin Wall, that horizontal monolith that divided not only a city between East and West but the world. At Checkpoint Charlie, the most famous point of entry into East Berlin, amid guard towers, machine guns, and an abundance of barbed wire, I surrendered my passport to one of the GDR soldiers on duty. He looked at the document, then up at me. "You are twenty minutes late for your appointment with Katarina Witt at the Steigenberger Hotel!"

Just imagine flying into JFK and having a customs official tell you that you're late for your meeting with Peggy Fleming at the Waldorf!

After our meeting, we headed over to Katarina's training rink in Karl-Marx-Stadt, the heart of the celebrated East German figure-skating program. As Betty Davis would say, "What a dump!" The arena was as bland and gray as the Berlin Wall itself. To create some sort of atmosphere for the sultry, romantic number "Hands to Heaven," we backlit shots to hide the arena walls, avoided wide shots, and limited framing to head-to-toes and close-ups.

Katarina defended her Olympic title in 1988 against another American challenger, Debi Thomas, in what was hyped as "The Battle of the Carmens" when the two chose the same Bizet composition for their long programs. The Berlin Wall came crumbling down the following year amid the euphoria of Glasnost, as did any remaining chilly walls around Katarina. She not only turned out to have a great sense of humor but freed herself in every sense of the word, best exemplified by her cover shoot and centerfold for *Playboy* magazine in 1998. When I later directed one of Katarina's TV specials, I facetiously grumbled about not having seen the magazine. She promised to send one. Time passed, and I reminded her a few times when we crossed paths at events. Finally, in 2004 at the World Championships in Dortmond, Katarina approached me with a mischievous smile on her face and handed me a large, white envelope. I knew what was inside and conjured up all sorts of fantasies about what she may have written in an inscription.

"With my love for you and your wonderful wife, Kat."

5

Score!

Early in my career, I was working on a program in ABC's TV-1 Studio that involved the ABC Symphony Orchestra. The crew had been working all morning completely focused on set design, lighting, camera angles, and framing. It was all about what appeared on the monitor, how the show would be seen. At lunch break, I emerged from the production control room, walked the narrow hallway, and glanced into the audio room. Wires were coming out of every available jack on the audio console. Crisscrossing, convoluted entanglements intertwined like spaghetti hanging over the edge of a bowl. Next to the panel of wire-filled confusion was the audio board, a gaggle of buttons and little lights and slide bars that seemed incredibly overwhelming to this mere production man.

The audio engineer responsible for this organized mess was Jack Kelly, who, incidentally, was the one who picked Leo Arnaud's "Bugler's Theme" for ABC's maiden Olympic telecast in 1964. This cavalry charge-sounding fanfare became known as the "Olympic Theme" and continues to be heard on Olympic telecasts today. Kelly had vacated his "office" for lunch, but left a handwritten cardboard sign prominently propped up on the console atop the coiled chaos. In large black marker it said, "Television is a visual medium."

Until you have seen a movie or video scene without sound, or even minus a few tracks of sound, you have no idea how much color and energy it adds to your viewing experience. Sound, especially music, isn't just an added effect. It's more than the audio frosting slapped on top of the video cake. It's what creates that sensational tingle when both ingredients combine.

Being a theater guy and a song-and-dance man wannabe, I often approached the creative part of producing a sporting event with music swimming through my mind. I discovered early in my career that when I married a music track to video of an athlete in motion, the athlete became a dancer; and when I added music to scenic footage, the drama heightened. The first time I recall employing music was for a tease for a *Wide World of Sports* episode in 1965. We created a soundtrack to accompany a party of climbers as they retraced the steps of the first successful, albeit tragic, summit of the Matterhorn that had occurred exactly one hundred years earlier.

I was flattered when Jim McKay used to tell people that I was the first to put sport to music on television. To me it was natural, second nature, but it was, to some degree, unprecedented in the early 1960s. NFL Films had begun to do similar creative work in the film medium at about the same time, and all credit is due to Leni Riefenstahl, Hitler's filmmaker. She was probably the first to choreograph brilliantly the movement of athletes to music in her famous film, *Olympia*, which documented the 1936 Games in Berlin.

There were two great women who worked in the ABC Music Library in New York, Lillian Gonfrade and Adele Irving. I often relied on their expertise to find the perfect song for a piece of action. I'd walk over to the library on West Sixty-Sixth Street and describe the feel of what I was looking for. When I was editing the footage for The Hustler's Tournament in 1965, for example, I described to Adele the Jansco Brothers' roadside bar off the main drag in a rural town in southern Illinois. I told her about pool sharks with names like "Boston Shorty" and "Handsome Danny from Detroit." Adele disappeared into the stacks and returned with the soundtrack album from Paul Newman's billiards movie, *The Hustler*. She recommended the cool but steamy sax number called "Sarah's Theme," which we used for our film-noirish intro. Starting from the backseat of a car, we framed the eerie silhouette of a man seated in front holding a pool cue case. The car then pulled off the road and up to the Jansco joint, where moving inside, we found Jim at the head of a pool table. He performed "Ya Got Trouble" from *The Music Man*: "You are not aware of the caliber of disaster indicated / By the presence of a pool table in your community!…" He then leaned over the table and drove six balls into the pockets with one stroke of the cue.

Lillian and Adele never failed me, and neither did the use of music. I always felt great creative joy putting together these teases, scene sets, and performances, and the feedback I received from colleagues and viewers was very gratifying. Below are a few of my favorites.

FOGGY DAY

In 1966, Muhammad Ali was set to defend his world heavyweight title against English boxer Brian London, a.k.a. "The British Bulldog," which aptly described both his fighting style and his flat-nosed face. The fight would take place in London. Chet Forte, who was producing the fight, asked me to open the telecast with Frank Sinatra's recording of "A Foggy Day (in London Town)." *Foggy Day*? I thought. *That's a love song! What would that have to do with a heavyweight fight*?

A week or so before we were to leave for England, Chet asked how the opening was coming along. "Great," I replied, though I'd done nothing but worry about it. When I got home that night and listened to the song one more time, a line of the lyrics jumped out at me: "How long, I wondered, could this thing last?"

That was funny! And even funnier when laid over Brian London's tired, grisly mug.

The entire shot list formed in comic strip-like captions popping above my head. I laid "What to do, what to do, what to do" over Ali standing on the steps of his hotel, looking this way and that. "As I walked through the dreary streets alone" went over Ali strolling in Soho with hundreds of people following him. The song turned out to be pure satire, playing against video images of the city's landmarks and the two contrasting personalities.

How long did the fight last? Not long. Ali knocked out London early in the third round. *Variety*'s review of our telecast noted that the fight wasn't all that entertaining but applauded the "Foggy Day" teaser: "Somebody at ABC Sports has a sense of style."

SYMPHONY NO. 9

As the Lauberhorn downhill ski race in the Swiss Alps was nearing in 1972, I pondered ways to communicate the dynamics of the longest downhill course on the World Cup circuit. The *average* grade of the 2.768-mile course is 14.7 degrees, so I thought that footage looking down from the top of the Empire State Building to Central Park in New York City would demonstrate the drop to our American viewers. Well, in order to accurately duplicate the Lauberhorn plunge, we'd have to put a second Empire State Building on top of the first, then put half of a third one on top of that! *That's* a World Cup or Olympic downhill!

When I first looked at the imposing panorama towering over the Lauberhorn course, I understood why it was called The Top of Europe. The Eiger, Mönch, and Jungfrau peaks would provide a spectacular backdrop for our broadcast. I wanted to capture this feeling of awe for our scene set. The question was, how?

I learned that a helicopter was available for hire in Wengen, a village at the base of the Eiger. As those were the days when I didn't have to worry about production costs, off I went with Dutch cameraman Eric van Haren Noman.

"Where do you want to go?" the pilot asked.

I pointed to the Eiger. "Up there. Can you fly above it?"

The Eiger, the shortest of the triumvirate, stood at 13,025 feet. The pilot said he could clear it by about 500 feet…his limit. So up we went, and I mean up. I felt my spine tingle and the goose bumps rise. Glorious. Absolutely glorious. I thought about Cole Porter's song "Wunderbar." The verse starts, "Gazing down on the Jungfrau from our secret chalet for two…" —I laughed. At 13,642 feet, the Jungfrau is the highest peak in the area. Nothing gazes down upon it! But we were about to, and Eric, strapped in and with his legs dangling out the open door, was about to record the view.

The Wengen side of the peaks was completely clear, but on the other side, a milky cloud layer covered the valley below as far as the eye could see. As we approached the Eiger, the pilot suddenly descended. Eric and I nervously glanced at each other. I figured something had to be wrong. We would crash on the treacherous north face and, in an attempt to self-rescue, would be swept off a ledge like Stefano Longhi, the climber McKay mentioned in our scene set, our frozen cadavers dangling from the precipice for years before being recovered!

The pilot made a controlled landing on a snowfield just below the top of the Mönch. With the rotors still spinning, he jumped out, got down on his hands and knees, and looked underneath the bird. He then climbed back in and took off. The din was so great there was no point in asking what was going on, and by the time we landed, I was so excited about the footage Eric had captured that I forgot to ask!

So what music would be as grand as those mountains itself? I didn't have to call Adele or Lillian for this one. I had known the perfect composition since I was twelve, when my brother David came home from Harvard one Christmas and played for me what he said was the greatest symphony of all time, Beethoven's Ninth.

My approach to recording sessions with Jim was always to have the music track in place before he screened the footage. This helped him feel the mood of the piece. We also played the music cut in his headset while he narrated because it inspired his delivery. This effect was never more evident than when the symphony's final movement, "Ode to Joy," played over Eric's soaring footage and Jim chimed in, "You're on top of the world! Above the Alps of Switzerland, looking down from a hovering helicopter as if suspended from a skyhook. Few men have even seen this area as you are seeing it now..."

A little footnote: producer Carol Lehti would thereafter use "Ode to Joy" as the traditional soundtrack to the credits crawl/highlights montage at the end of all of our Olympic broadcasts.

EAST MEETS WEST

The power of the international language of music was never more clearly demonstrated than during a gymnastics meet that took place between the United States and the People's Republic of China in 1973.

Today's younger generations may not be fully aware of the depth of America's hostile relationship with China after Mao Tse-tung established it as a Communist state in 1949. China had been our staunch ally against Imperial Japan during World War II but fought against us during the Korean War, which started in 1950. All communication between our countries ceased, and Chairman Mao fanned the flames of anti-American hatred throughout the population.

By the time *Wide World of Sports* went on the air in 1961, China and the United States were deadly enemies. Relations between the two countries began to warm ten years later when China invited the US table tennis team to play in China. The players became the first Americans to set foot in China since the revolution. These exhibition matches, which became known as Ping-Pong Diplomacy, cracked open the door that led to the visit by President Nixon in early 1972. Nixon was the first US president to visit the People's Republic of China. A couple of months later, the Chinese team toured the Unites States, and in 1973, the Chinese gymnasts dropped by New York for some friendly competition.

The American crowd in Madison Square Garden applauded all the athletes with equal vigor. Then, as American Nancy Thies began her floor exercise, the audiotape malfunctioned. The technicians tried again. No music. Now what? It just so happened that the music for Chinese gymnasts was not recorded but played live by a pianist. In desperation, Muriel Grossfeld, the American coach, approached the Chinese accompanist, Chou Chia-sheng. He wore a Mao suit, like everyone else in the Chinese delegation, and did not speak a word of English. On the monitors in the control room, we watched with amusement as Muriel gestured repeatedly as she and an interpreter tried to explain Nancy's routine to the pianist.

Nancy returned to the mat. She started her performance; Chia-sheng started his improvisation. Bill Flemming commented that it was as if a librettist had brought some words to a composer and said, "Let's see how it works out." Well, it was brilliant. Chia-sheng anticipated every movement, every maneuver. It looked as if they had rehearsed for weeks!

"A gal from Urbana and a man from Peking," observed expert commentator Gordon Maddux—the "twain" that Kipling said shall never meet were inseparable as they performed together. As Nancy eased into her final pose, Chia-sheng complemented it with a glissando. The crowd erupted thunderously. Everyone present understood that the discord of political adversaries had been silenced, if only temporarily, by music and sport.

6

Sound Bites

As I traveled around the planet, I got to see with my own eyes all those amazing sights our camera crews recorded: the eagle's eye views of the Eiger, the rugged hills of California's Gold Country, the cityscape of historic Vienna, and the full three-hundred-mile stretch of the mighty Hudson River from the Statue of Liberty to the headwaters high in the Adirondack Mountains. And the *sounds*! I heard *live* the church bells of St. Moritz echoing through the Engadin Valley, a performance of *Carmen* by the Teatro dell'Opera di Roma at the magnificent ruins of the Baths of Caracalla, and the screeching of a Ferrari GT in the dark of night at Le Mans as it geared down from two hundred miles an hour to thirty to make the treacherous turn at the end of the Mulsanne Straight. I saw and heard many wondrous things, but often, surprisingly, my most treasured keepsakes were simply the things people said.

CRAPS

I was in Las Vegas in 1968 for the annual Professional Bowlers Tour stop at the Showboat Hotel & Casino. I had a few hours to kill before our production meeting, so I wandered into the Thunderbird Hotel, one of the original resorts on the Strip. The casino was unusually quiet, almost surreal because the only other patron was a man seated on a barstool about fifteen feet away. Sonny Liston, of all people. He wasn't playing. He just sat there, staring into space, and looking scary, despite the porkpie hat on his head.

I wasn't much of a gambler but had watched Chet Forte play craps many times while on location, with thousands of dollars going in and out of his hands (he eventually became active in Gamblers Anonymous). He and others had told me that craps was the best game, had the best odds, and was the most fun. We've all seen it in the movies: the suave guy blowing the dice in his hand for luck, offering them to the exquisite woman beside him for a kiss, then the gathered revelers cheering as the tiny cubes carom down the green felt.

I approached the one open table and introduced myself to the croupier. I told him I was with ABC Sports—always a good conversation starter—and that I wanted to learn how to play craps. He was delighted to show me.

First, he asked for money. In exchange for a twenty, he placed some chips on a square on the playing surface. He then handed me the dice and told me to throw them. I didn't win, didn't lose. No cheering revelers, either. He then said something about rolling the same number before rolling a seven or an eleven, and told me to roll again. Again, no consequence. I think I was supposed to roll the same number I had rolled first, but that didn't happen.

I rolled again.

"You lost."

He raked away my chips with that crooked little stick in his hand. Money gone.

"That's the way the game is played," he said seriously, but with a hint of a smile. "Never come back."

COSELL

I had just been promoted to producer when I crossed paths with Howard Cosell at corporate headquarters. He stopped, put his arm around my shoulders, looked down at me, and said in that unique voice of his, pausing between every word and placing emphasis and enthusiasm on every other syllable, "*Doug Wil*-son! Young *man* of man-y *fac*-e-ted *tal*-ents, un-*bounded* im-*ag*-i-*na*-tion, you're *go*-ing to *go* a *long* way *in...this... bus*-iness."

I was flattered—Howard Cosell did not commonly give compliments. I looked up at him (because I was only five feet seven and a half inches and balding, and he was six feet two with his hair piece) and said, "Thanks, Coach, but I'll always live in your shadow."

"My boy," he said, "that's im-*pos*-si-ble. I...*cast...no...sha*-dow!"

WOODY

In 1969 and 1970, I produced the telecast of one of the classic, most legendary of all collegiate football rivalries, the regular season-ending game between the University of Michigan Wolverines and The Ohio State University Buckeyes. This Big Ten Conference clash was always contentious, and this one would become the first in a series that would later be known as The Ten Year War between Buckeye head coach Woody Hayes and Wolverine head coach Bo Schembechler. The larger-than-life Hayes was infamous for being temperamental (in 1978, he would be fired for punching a Clemson Tiger in the throat after making a game-saving interception), and in 1969, emotions were dialed up further because Schembechler had been one of Hayes's assistants earlier in his career.

During a pregame interview on the sideline of Michigan Stadium in Ann Arbor, announcer Bill Flemming said to Hayes, "They say you're a man of no mercy." He was referring to the criticism that had been launched at Hayes for running up scores against lesser teams. Hayes replied, "Frankly, I don't care much what they think. I know this...we would like to be the best team in this nation. There's been talk about our being the best team of the century, and I'm not going to hold my kids back."

Ohio State lost 24 to 12.

The following year, Woody Hayes made a brief appearance at the traditional night-before-the-big-game dinner hosted by a wealthy Buckeye supporter. Hayes began by thanking everyone for their support and, of course, talked up victory the following day on the gridiron. Then, in the wake of 1967's "Summer of Love" and 1969's Woodstock, Hayes concluded, "Gentlemen, I'm reminded of the good old days, when the air was clean and sex was dirty!"

KING OF THE HILL

Austrian ski racer Karl Schranz, considered by many to be the greatest downhill racer of all time, was favored to win the Lauberhorn in 1972. During an interview we taped a few weeks before the event, Jim asked Schranz if he was ever afraid while standing in the start gate at the top of a course.

"I have never felt fear in my life," Schranz replied in a heavy German-Austrian accent.

The weather was warm as the day of the downhill approached. The upper part of the course was bare in spots, and rocks poked through the thin layer of snow. As the practice runs were concluding, the racers gathered around Schranz just beyond the finish line. As the patriarch, he opined that the course was too dangerous for racing.

"Jungle Jim" Hunter, the youngest member of the Canadian team, skied onto the scene. He had earned his nickname for his aggressive style. He was also known as the original "Crazy Canuck," perhaps for practicing his tuck while strapped to a rack on the roof of a truck that his father was driving at one hundred kilometers per hour!

"You don't want to race?" Jungle Jim crowed. "We came to race. If you don't want to race, go home!"

Schranz paused. The "King of Mount Arlberg" looked the kid up and down and said, "Ohhhh, you must be very good."

STUD FARM

Lucien Laurin trained Riva Ridge, the Thoroughbred that won the 1972 Kentucky Derby and Belmont Stakes. I was in Kentucky to document the horse's training regimen for *Wide World* when Lucien took me to a stud farm. As we drove in and passed bucolic pastures where mares and their foals were recreating in the open spaces, it struck me that there was not a single stallion in sight. I mentioned this to Lucien.

He turned to me and smiled. "A stallion is good for one thing and a mare for another!"

HIGH SPEED

Wide World of Sports first televised the Firecracker 250 at Daytona Beach in 1961, which gave Bill France Sr.'s Southern-based National Association for Stock Car Auto Racing a national television audience. I began producing NASCAR telecasts in the late 1960s and felt there was something deeply American and "working man" about stock car racing. After all, the sport had its roots in legends like Fireball Roberts and Junior Johnson. Johnson apparently learned his racing skills in cars loaded with bootlegged moonshine while outrunning "revenuers"—Federal tax agents—through the back roads of North Carolina's red clay country in the late 1940s and 1950s.

In 1969, Bill France Sr. opened the Alabama International Motor Speedway, now known as the Talladega Superspeedway. It was bigger and faster than Daytona and would be NASCAR's answer to the Indy 500. ABC Sports was invited to survey the new track for upcoming television coverage. I got the assignment, and so it was that I would meet Bill France Jr., who would take over the reins of NASCAR in 1972 and turn stock car racing into the significant and lucrative part of American culture it is today.

Bill Jr. was also a licensed pilot. He picked me up one morning in a twin-engine plane at Westchester County Airport in New York. About an hour and a half into the flight, he landed in Winston-Salem so he could take me to his favorite barbecue stand for lunch. In a rented car, we headed out of town a few miles, then turned down a dirt road into the Carolina woods. After we enjoyed the Southern-style fixin's at a wooden shack with open sides, Bill was back behind the wheel—and let 'er fly. Sure enough, a siren started up behind us. Unshaken, Bill pulled over.

The state trooper arrived at the driver's window. "License and registration, please."

Bill handed him the documents. The officer looked them over.

"You're *Bill France*? Bill France from *NASCAR*?"

Bill broke into a little smile, confident that his legendary name would ease him out of the predicament.

The officer flipped open his pad.

"I can't wait to tell my family at dinner tonight that I gave a speeding ticket to Bill France!"

RAQUEL

Upon my arrival in Canada in 1972 to produce ABC's second telecast of the Calgary Stampede, Bill Pratt, the general manager of the Stampede, called me into his office. He told me that he felt that ABC's inaugural coverage the prior year was the reason they had cleared a million people at the gate for the first time. To show his appreciation, Bill presented me with a fine Stetson cowboy hat. The hat became part of my "uniform," complementing my collection of cowboy boots. It also became very handy at remotes, making me easy to find in a crowd.

Several years later, Gary Smith, with whom I had worked on Dorothy Hamill's television special, approached me regarding working with him and Dwight Hemion on a Raquel Welch special to be taped in Rio de Janeiro during Carnival. Welch, an iconic sex symbol/movie star in the United States and who was half Latina, was hugely popular in Brazil.

I met Ms. Welch in the Pan Am first class lounge shortly before boarding the plane in New York. When we landed in Rio, I disembarked with her, my Stetson shielding me from the equatorial sun. The paparazzi were waiting. The next day, the front page of the one newspaper that continued to publish during Carnival featured a picture of Raquel Welch and an "unidentified stranger accompanying her, wearing a cowboy hat."

The next evening when we left the hotel for the parade, a thousand or more fans were waiting outside, eager to get a glimpse of the star. I was wearing a coat and tie for the occasion, and Ms. Welch was stunning in a black, sleeveless cocktail dress that adorned her gorgeous figure. She was also wearing a brilliant diamond necklace and earrings that a local jeweler had loaned her earlier that day. The crowd was aggressive and unruly, hands reaching out to touch her.

"I'm scared," she said to me.

I put my arm around her waist. "Don't worry," I said, trying not to think about the fact that *my* arm was around *Raquel Welch's* waist! "You'll be OK." We safely cleared our way through the mob and into the waiting limousine.

After ducking through back alleys and passageways, and watching a slinky celebrity climb over scaffolding pipes in high heels, we made it to the VIP stands. While Ms. Welch chatted with the mayor, I stepped away to get some refreshments. When I returned, she took the lime-colored Caipirinha cocktail from my hand, gave me the once-over, and smiled.

"Where's your fucking cowboy hat?"

GRAMMAR LESSON

Howard Cosell and Jim McKay had a complex relationship. They had mutual respect for each other, but Cosell was always envious of McKay's universal popularity, which may explain why he often—and publically— referred to Jim, who was short in stature, as "the diminutive one." On the other hand, McKay was deferential to Cosell's charisma. Cosell had opinions and never hesitated to voice them. He made no apologies for his loquaciousness, often proclaiming a phrase that became his mantra: "I'm telling it like it is."

On more than one occasion, McKay turned to me and corrected Cosell's grammar sotto voce, "*as* it is."

SECRETARIAT

The magnificent Secretariat won the Triple Crown in 1973 and was celebrated across the country like a movie star. He was set to race a few weeks later at Arlington Park just outside Chicago, and ABC Sports had garnered the rights to the live telecast. As producer, I wanted our coverage to include some novel production techniques. We were the first to use a handheld camera on the track at the start of a horse race. We also put mikes on Lucien Laurin, Secretariat's trainer, and Penny Chenery Tweedy, Secretariat's winsome owner, the mother of four who took over her father's Thoroughbred farm at age forty-five. I remember how hard Mrs. Tweedy tried to be analytical during the race, but as Secretariat passed the half-mile pole and was fending off a challenge from My Gallant, all she could muster was "Com'on, big boy!" When her Big Red finally pulled away in the backstretch, she hollered, "Wooo!"

Before the race, I asked Sam Renick, former jockey and our racing expert, what it was about Secretariat's anatomy that made him the greatest racehorse of his time, if not all time. Sam said that the horse's muscular chest and huge nostrils allowed him to inhale more oxygen (after he died, an autopsy revealed that Secretariat's heart was two times the average size). We created a diagram to illustrate the horse's superior physiognomy, but this was television. I thought it would be more effective to stand next to the actual horse and point out these attributes. Arrangements were made with the handlers to have Secretariat stop for us in the paddock before the race. Timing would be critical, as our window of opportunity would be no more than one minute. Roone would be coordinating the show from New York, which had four elements: the Queen's Plate horse race live from Toronto, the NCAA Volleyball Championships on tape from San Diego, a live segment on All-Star pitcher Gaylord Perry's alleged spitball, and, finally, our race from Illinois.

Unfortunately, New York came to us about a minute late. Well, you can't hold up a horse race. Although Secretariat's groom, Eddie Sweat, had stopped the horse as planned and was ready beside Sam for the interview, the parade started moving again. When commentator Chris Schenkel was finally able to throw it over to Sam from the booth, Sweat couldn't wait any longer. He, Secretariat, and jockey Ron Turcotte moved out of frame. Sam chased Turcotte through the crowd, his mike cable dragging behind him from beneath his yellow blazer. Turcotte then mounted the horse and proceeded toward the track. Sam literally reached the end of his rope when the camera cable could stretch no further.

On screen, instead of our viewers seeing Secretariat's enormous nostrils and chest, they saw his equally enormous derriere plodding away from the camera as Sam, desperately trying to save the botched interview, blurted, "Secretariat never looked better in his life!"

WELL PRESERVED

In late 1979, two-time Olympic and four-time World champion pair skaters Oleg Protopopov and Lyudmila Belousova defected from the Soviet Union to Switzerland. During their reign in the 1960s, this husband/wife team was considered the greatest pair of all time. They enhanced their skating with ballet and, in doing so, changed their sport forever and became the first in a long line of superlative Soviet pair skaters.

The Protopopovs are famous for having created three variations of the death spiral, a move so named because if the woman, who is leaning extremely deeply on one edge, loses her partner's grip, her head will slam into the ice. On one occasion, Oleg corrected my terminology with his admonishment, "Ve do not do a death spiral, ve do a *life* spiral." Although these spirals were dramatic moves to watch, my favorite was their hand-to-hand lasso, where Oleg lifted Lyudmila over his head, as she balanced on the end of his fully extended arm, then soared across the ice like an eagle in flight.

Shortly after their defection, I met the Protopopovs at a private skating facility on Long Island. My assignment was to shoot a few segments for our upcoming Olympic telecast from Lake Placid. Oleg and Lyudmila were in their fifties then but were still skating in top form. After working all day, we sat down for an interview. I asked Oleg how they were able to separate their marriage from their skating. He paused, then eyed me with great intensity, raising one finger in front of my face.

"Our skatingz and our marriage—zay are one!"

I then turned to Lyudmila and asked her what was the secret to their longevity as world-class skaters. Through large glasses that made her attractive eyes appear even wider, she said, "We are always in the refrigerator."

TORVILL & DEAN

Jayne Torvill and Christopher Dean's 1984 free skate for the gold medal in ice dancing stunned people everywhere. The two Brits mesmerized us with both their technical ability—receiving unprecedented 6.0s from every single judge—and their chemistry, which sizzled in a very sexually charged rendition of Ravel's "Bolero." The choice to use only one piece of music for a skating program (usually there are three) created a challenge in that the beat and tempo would never change. Furthermore, this particular piece of music repeats the same melody over and over. Even the composer called it "incessant." Ravel made "Bolero" hypnotic and riveting by layering instruments at it progressed, building a titillating intensity. Torvill and Dean's choreography had the same effect.

This performance was clearly the climax of the Olympic competition in Sarajevo, and the two skaters became the center of a global media frenzy. Everyone wanted to know everything about them and whether they were romantically involved because they had to be in order to do what they did on the ice (they were not). The attention was so fanatical that Dean said, "The only time Jayne and I have any privacy is when we are on the ice in front of thousands of people."

WHITAKER

The Kentucky Derby, "The Greatest Two Minutes in Sports," is to horse racing what the Masters is to golf. It's more than just a horse race. It is a deeply ingrained American happening, having begun way back in 1875. Celebrities abound, and gentry in seersucker suits and fancy hats mingle with shirtless, jean-clad youth to celebrate the mid-spring sunshine. Its signature moment is not the rush when the gates whip open and the horses dart forward but rather that magical time during the post parade when the horses are led onto the track. The live band plays the Derby's historic anthem, Stephen Foster's "My Old Kentucky Home," and thousands of balloons rise into the sky. Many spectators sing along, while others raise their mint juleps to honor the spirit and tradition of this classic sporting event.

During a preview show a week before the race in the 1980s, announcer Jack Whitaker stood outside the railing at the first turn where ABC would place a camera. Jack described the thundering Thoroughbreds viewers would see pounding toward that camera angle at the start of the "Run for the Roses." Then, he paused. "And next week, when the band strikes up 'My Old Kentucky Home' and the balloons are released into the heavens, if you don't have a tear in your eye…you ought to be ashamed of yourself."

SI JINX

Shortly before the Calgary Olympics, Bill Taaffe wrote a favorable article for *Sports Illustrated* about my directing methods and how I would use the cameras to enhance Brian Boitano's Olympic program. In expressing my gratitude to Bill, I asked if this came under the *SI* "Kiss of Death" superstition, where great athletes and teams who have been touted by the magazine then see their winning streaks broken, become seriously ill or paralyzed, lose their next competition, or their lives, as happened with several race car drivers.

"Don't worry," Bill told me. "That only happens when you're on the cover."

GOLD MEDAL

Figure-skating champion Scott Hamilton always seemed to push back adversity with a buoyant spirit. As a child, he had an undiagnosed condition that slowed his growth and development and prevented him from absorbing food normally. Still, Scott wore a smile underneath the feeding tubes in his nose that delivered nutrients directly to his digestive system, as depicted in a photograph we showed on the air many times. When Scott started skating, the problems went away, and he finally felt on equal footing with other kids, who had always left him for last when picking teams on the school playground because he was small. But that didn't stop him. By age twenty-six, Scott racked up four US and three World Championships, then won Olympic gold in 1984. During an interview when he first splashed onto the international scene, Scott joked that he still had to buy sport coats "with Donald Duck on the pocket" and knew he'd "never be able to date Susan Anton" (the beautiful, six-foot-tall TV and film star at the time).

Only once did I see Scott leave the ice without a smile, and it happened on the night he won the gold. Scott had such a strong lead going into the long program that when he popped open on his second jump and later downgraded a triple to a double, Dick Button reminded our viewers that neither mistake would hurt him. Though the crowd cheered throughout the rest of Scott's otherwise excellent program, he was crestfallen as he stepped off the ice, turned to his coach, and said, "Sorry."

As Scott's life progressed to professional competition and ice-show stardom, health issues hit him again. In 1997, Scott was diagnosed with testicular cancer, which he overcame. In 2004, he learned he had a brain tumor. The tumor, which apparently was the cause of his childhood illness, was giving him terrible headaches and putting pressure on his ocular nerves. In a phone conversation prior to surgery, I asked Scott how he was feeling.

"Well," he said, "I feel sorry for you."

"Really?"

"Yeah. When you look at a beautiful woman, you see only one. I see one and a half!"

The crew setting up at Las Vegas Invitational Sky
Diving in 1963. "Everything we did was new..."
© American Broadcasting Companies, Inc.

Roone Arledge and the "tyrannical device" in the control
room of the 1980 Winter Olympics in Lake Placid.
© American Broadcasting Companies, Inc.

Jim McKay in the Munich Olympic Stadium in
1972 before "all hell broke loose."
© American Broadcasting Companies, Inc.

Evel Knievel, the father of extreme sports, on the launch pad for the Snake River Canyon jump, 1974. © American Broadcasting Companies, Inc.

Muhammad Ali and Howard Cosell nose to nose in an ABC Studio circa 1975. Cosell always referred to their interviews as "sparring sessions." © American Broadcasting Companies, Inc.

Muhammad Ali, Ronnie Hawkins, and Doug Wilson working
together at ABC in New York after Ali's fight with Quarry, 1970.
© American Broadcasting Companies, Inc.

Scott Hamilton skates to Olympic
gold in Sarajevo, 1984.
© American Broadcasting
Companies, Inc.

Nadia Comaneci scores the first perfect 10 in gymnastics
at the Montreal Olympics in 1976.
© American Broadcasting Companies, Inc.

Doug having a laugh with the 20th century's two famous crashers, Evel Knievel and
Vinko Bogataj, at "*ABC's Wide World of Sports* 25th Anniversary Special" in 1986.
© American Broadcasting Companies, Inc.

Vinko Bogataj tumbles into fame as "the agony of defeat guy" at the Ski
Flying Championships in Oberstdorf, West Germany in 1970.
Courtesy ABC Sports, Inc.

Arthur Ashe, 1974, a champion both on and off the court.
© American Broadcasting Companies, Inc.

Arthure Ashe wearing
the iconic yellow ABC
Sports blazer.
© American Broadcasting
Companies, Inc.

Crazy Canuck "Jungle Jim" Hunter in training.
As seen in *The Sword of the Lord*.
© 1976 National Film Board of Canada. All rights reserved.

Karl Schranz winning the Lauberhorn downhill in Wengen, Austria, 1966.
Courtesy of Karl Schranz

Cameraman Bill Sullivan rehearses with Oleg Protopopov and Lyudmila
Belousova on Long Island, New York shortly after their defection from
the Soviet Union. ABC aired an "Up Close and Personal" segment
about the couple during its 1980 Winter Olympics coverage.
Photo by Harriet Hochberg

Peggy Fleming and Doug mimic a sculpture of the
Protopopovs in St. Petersburg, Russia, 1994.
Photo by Meg Streeter-Lauck

Jim McKay, his son Sean McManus (now chairman of CBS Sports), and Doug at a water skiing competition at Cypress Gardens, Florida in the mid-1960s. © American Broadcasting Companies, Inc.

Genuine Risk comes from behind to win the Kentucky Derby, 1980.
© American Broadcasting Companies, Inc.

Olga Korbut becomes a household name during the sublime first week of the 1972 Munich Summer Games. © American Broadcasting Companies, Inc.

An ABC Sports television camera catches a Palestinian terrorist peeking from the apartment of the Olympic Village where the Israeli team members are being held hostage and a German policeman on the roof. ABC's exclusive, live coverage of the Munich tragedy brought the reality and horror of terrorism right into the living rooms of millions of Americans. Courtesy ABC Sports, Inc.

A rider hangs on for control through the infamous
Shuttlecock turn of the Cresta Run in St. Moritz.
Courtesy of fotoswiss.com/giancarlocattaneo

Doug, Dorothy Hamill, and
Chuck Mangione planning
Dorothy's Closing Ceremony
performance for the 1984
Lake Placid Olympics.
© American Broadcasting
Companies, Inc.

Billie Jean King and Bobby Riggs make nice before the historical "Battle of the Sexes" in Houston, 1973. © American Broadcasting Companies, Inc.

Jim McKay with Formula One champion Stirling Moss at the Daytona 500, 1962. © American Broadcasting Companies, Inc.

Dorothy Hamill competes in the 1976 Winter Olympics in Innsbruck, Austria. Beneath the joy, there was always deep determination. © American Broadcasting Companies, Inc.

Nadia Comaneci, fit and unbeatable, at the Tokyo World Cup in 1979. Courtesy of International Gymnast Magazine

Doug and Brian Boitano plan coverage of Brian's free skate program at Nationals in Denver, 1988. © Heinz Kluetmeier/ Sports Illustrated Classic/Getty Images

Brian Boitano on his way to the title at the 1988 US Figure Skating Championships in Denver. © American Broadcasting Companies, Inc.

Brian Boitano warms up in the Alaskan wilderness for his primetime special "Canvas of Ice," October, 1988. Photo by Lydia Murphy-Stephans

Michelle Kwan performs her signature spiral at the World Figure Skating Championships in Philadelphia in 1998. Olympic gold eluded this nine-time National and five-time World champion, but she showed us all that the true mark of a champion is how she conducts herself in both victory and defeat. © American Broadcasting Companies, Inc.

Technical director John Zipay and Doug face the monitor wall in the early 2000s.
Photo by Jack Morris

Evel Knievel breaks a few more bones in Wembley Stadium, 1975.
Photo by Harry Ormesher.

Peggy Fleming glides in the chartreuse dress her mother made for her. Peggy made it famous while winning a gold medal at the 1968 Winter Olympics in Grenoble. © American Broadcasting Companies, Inc.

The ABC team at the 1976 Winter Olympics in Innsbruck, Austria.
© American Broadcasting Companies, Inc.

7

Vignettes from the Voyage

Just by showing up for work, I regularly saw people do extraordinary things. But what was most noteworthy about many of the athletes and colleagues with whom I worked wasn't that they won titles in thrilling fashion or made brilliant calls on the air or raised millions of dollars for noble causes. Often what made these people remarkable to me was when they did something unexpected, even ordinary.

THE BOXER

I attended my first professional boxing match when Mike Stokey, the host of *Pantomime Quiz* (the first charades-inspired game show on television), handed me tickets to the second Floyd Patterson vs. Ingemar Johansson bout. The Polo Grounds, New York City, June 20, 1960. What a night. There's truly nothing in sports like a heavyweight championship fight. Celebrities were seated all around me, and in the ring were two men about to go at it like Roman gladiators. The bell sounds and fists fly, sweat pours, blood gushes…OK, so boxing is barbaric, but at least the ultimate defeat in ancient times, death, has been replaced by the more civilized knockout.

Patterson lost his first encounter with the Swede, who called his right fist the "Hammer of Thor," and the American was not favored to turn things around in the rematch. But in the fifth round, *pow*! Johansson went down. I was looking right at the soles of his boxing boots. The ten count went by, and he still lay there, his left foot twitching from the trauma generated by Patterson's blows. It was eerie to watch.

In 1974, I was returning from a motocross event in Scandinavia and had an airline connection in Bergen, Norway. I recognized Patterson sitting in the waiting room. He was alone, so I said hello. He told me that he had been in Sweden visiting his friend, Ingemar. I smiled and mentioned that I was at their second fight. To my further delight, Mr. Patterson was seated next to me on the plane. I was surprised to find that such a punishing pugilist with such a crushing hook could be so gentle and soft-spoken—now I understood why he was called the "Gentleman of Boxing." Patterson reminisced about his friendship with Johansson and his boxing career, then the in-flight movie began. It was called *Limbo* and was about several military wives awaiting the fate of their husbands who had been lost in combat in Vietnam. The movie did not end on a happy note. The wife the audience most wants to see reunited with her spouse learns that hers has been killed.

The credits rolled and the lights in the cabin flickered on. I glanced toward Patterson and saw the former heavyweight champion of the world, the man who made Ingemar Johansson's feet twitch, sitting quietly with his head slightly bowed and tears rolling down his cheeks.

MRS. SHRIVER

She was worried because her brother Jack had told her never to give a speech before a ball game. "People don't want to hear a speech," he said. "They've come to watch the game!" But there she stood, right where the late president of the United States told her never to be: at home plate standing before a microphone and a sell-out crowd.

Eunice Kennedy Shriver was in Yankee Stadium in the summer of 1979 to recognize Ron Guidry for his support of the Special Olympics, which she had founded during the prior decade. Like Shriver, the Cy Young Award-winning pitcher had a sibling with mental retardation and got involved with the organization to help the cause for people like his younger brother. I was on hand that day because of my *Wide World of Sports* assignment to produce the telecast of the International Special Olympics that would take place a couple of weeks later at The College at Brockport.

Despite Mrs. Shriver's concerns, the Guidry presentation was warmly received by the fans. It also maximized interest in the Brockport event. After Guidry's grateful response, we were all escorted to George Steinbrenner's box behind and above home plate to watch the game. The infamous Yankee owner was not in his box that day, and Mrs. Shriver wasn't the type to sit around and watch baseball when there were things to be done. She wanted to visit the group of Special Olympians who, to her dismay, had been assigned seats way out in the left-field upper deck. So off we went.

While in the walkway under the stadium, a small boy who looked about nine years old tried to approach Mrs. Shriver. We positioned ourselves to keep her moving through the vomitorium and out to the seats to join the Olympians. I confess to having felt somewhat tense about meeting them. I was a little afraid of mentally challenged people. I wasn't sure how to act or talk with someone who, for example, had Down syndrome. I was watching Mrs. Shriver interact so naturally with all the athletes, when I felt a hand gently rest on my shoulder. I turned around and found myself looking into the happiest, friendliest face I had ever seen. He was a Special Olympian with Down syndrome who just wanted to say hello. From that moment on, the production project became a labor of love for me.

About a half hour later, Mrs. Shriver rose to leave, and out of nowhere came the little lad who had tried to get to her earlier. I didn't think the boy was part of the Special Olympics contingent because I hadn't seen him sitting with the group, and when we had encountered him under the stadium, he was by himself. He likely recognized Mrs. Shriver from the Guidry speech as someone of importance. Smart kid. On his second attempt, he caught Mrs. Shriver's eye. She stopped, and as the boy began to speak, she stooped down to listen closely. Only Mrs. Shriver could hear what he said. When the boy finished, Mrs. Shriver straightened up and asked if anyone had a pencil and paper. Someone handed her a pencil. No one had paper, so I picked up a discarded popcorn box, tore off a piece, and handed it to her. She wrote something on the cardboard, handed it to the boy, and said in her Boston accent, "Now, young man, this is my address. You must write me a lettah. Do you understand? You must write me a lettah, and if you do, I will see to it that you learn how to swim."

HUMBLE HOWARD

Although Howard Cosell's "tell it like it is" commentary made him both charismatic and controversial, I have often wondered if his infamous bravado was emboldened by alcohol. This was a man who, after some hours in the narration recording booth, would call out to me, "Doogie, Doogie, where's my vodka?" I always tried to delay the delivery as long as possible and then made sure there was a lot of ice. Back in 1981, I received a phone call from Al Michaels that convinced me that Howard's commentary was occasionally "inspired." Al was calling from Kansas City, where he would be covering the Royals/Yankees game on *Monday Night Baseball* with Howard that night. He didn't call to talk about the game, though. He wanted to tell me about something that had happened the night before. After a late dinner, during which Howard had consumed his usual libations, the two were on their way back to their hotel when their limo stopped at a red light in a dangerous part of town. Al said that Howard noticed three young black men circled around two others who were fighting. Howard asked the driver, Peggy, to turn down the street. She said it wasn't a good idea, not to mention she'd be going the wrong way on a one-way street. Howard insisted.

The car crept to within fifteen feet of the threatening scene. The fight halted, and all eyes locked on the ominous black sedan looming in the shadows. Despite Al's attempts to stop him, Howard opened the limo door and walked into the fray like a lone wolf sheriff strutting into town, his fingers wrapped around a long, slender cigar instead of a Colt .45.

Shouting analytical Cosell-eze, Howard derided the skills of the combatants and declared, "I'm ending this fight *right now!*"

For a moment, it seemed that the men might attack.

"Howard Cosell! It's Howard Cosell!" one of them exclaimed, embracing the toupee'd intruder. The others went nuts, surrounding the famous sportscaster who was well respected in the black community for his championing of civil rights. Howard held court with the guys for a few minutes, signed some autographs, then returned to the limo. Peggy rapidly drove off, remarking that she had "never seen anything like that... ever."

Cosell sat back, took a long draw on his cigar..."Peggy-roo, I know-who-I-am!"

CANVAS OF ICE

Camera five, the reverse angle, caught the moment as the theme from *Napoleon and Josephine* concluded. Looking rather dignified in a military-inspired costume with gold brocade on the shoulders and collar, Brian Boitano struck a victorious pose, thrusting one arm into the air and the other across his waist. Already smiling as he transitioned from his performance persona to a twenty-five-year-old who had just skated the program of his life, Brian clenched his fists and euphorically looked heavenward.

Although Brian's long program at the Calgary Olympics in 1988 was the culmination of his competitive career, he would skate to new heights in his ABC TV special, "Canvas of Ice." Shortly after winning his gold medal, Brian told me he wanted to skate on a glacier in Alaska. There we were eight months later in the darkness of predawn Anchorage, rising each morning to drive three and a half hours into the wilderness. Our staging area was a lonely cabin, occupied by a solitary old man who thought we were all crazy. We had learned about the place through our Canadian production manager, David Rhines, who had also hired a bush pilot to scope out our ultimate destination.

The sun rose to reveal a glorious day, the first of three—unusual for Alaska during the fall. A helicopter thundered in from the azure sky, and I climbed aboard for the second trip to the production site. We flew like a bird past blue ice flows, then lifted over a sizable hill. There it appeared... an alpine lake. The entire scene was so remote, so pristine, I wondered if we were the first to ever visit. About a third of the frozen expanse was covered with a thin layer of snow that had crusted in the sun. Sitting in the center was Sandra Bezic, Brian's choreographer and former Canadian Pairs Champion, soaking up the sun, her blonde locks contrasting against the translucent black ice. I knew as I surveyed the entire panorama that we were about to record something special.

We unloaded our gear, and the production crew started to place cameras and music playback speakers, hiding them in the hillsides and the embankment surrounding the lake. We then rehearsed two numbers, one to David Foster's reflective instrumental "Water Fountain," and a second to Bruce Broughton's adventurous theme from the movie *Silverado*. Both compositions were suitable to the surroundings, one expressing serenity and the other majesty.

With the crew ready, the helicopter above, and cameraman extraordinaire Darcy March in our old friend the wheelchair (pushed by Sandra), Brian set out on his canvas. On TV, the scenery looked like an inviting, crystal-clear, early winter landscape with relatively mild temperatures in the low thirties Fahrenheit. In reality, it was in the teens, and the wind chill dropped the numbers to below zero. Brian was vulnerable, yet he strove for perfection in take after take, axel after axel, and Tano after Tano—his trademark triple Lutz—an already difficult jump made even more so because he extended his left arm above his head while doing it. In between takes, we defrosted Brian beside a Coleman heater, wrapping him in space blankets and rubbing his legs. Those Olympic thighs were as solid as iron I beams on the Fifty-Ninth Street Bridge!

Once we completed shooting the *Silverado* number, I asked Brian if he would move into the expanse of crusted snow and simply skate with abandon for a couple of minutes. The result was a breathtaking climax to our show. From the helicopter's eagle eye, the viewer saw the Olympic champion's tiny, carefree silhouette glide across the snow and ice, kicking up powder that swirled and glistened in the wind, while the setting sun created dramatic long shadows that seemed to play along.

I have always felt that music drives the train in figure skating. It is the connection, the bridge that carries the skater's emotions through the choreography, into the cameras, and out to the viewers. But in this scenario, there was a third element: the environment. A powerful visual moment came during "Water Fountain" when Brian performed a spectacular spread eagle. As he began the maneuver, Sandra pushed the wheelchair camera into position behind him, then pivoted to follow his giant arc on the ice. This enabled viewers to see what Brian saw as he leaned back on his outside edges and raised his eyes and arms in reverence to the 360 degrees of Alaskan wonder surrounding him.

A pensive and quiet interlude followed. Brian, Sandra, Darcy, and I gathered in the center of the pond to discuss the choreography for this section. Our conclusion was that Brian merely pause during those bars and look around, absorbing the breathtaking landscape. Brian would later tell me how spiritually connected he felt to the environment out there on that frozen lake. It certainly showed in his skating. He filled his canvas of ice with extraordinary artistry during our three days in the Alaskan frontier, but his finest moment of expression emerged when he simply stood still.

8

The Cresta

Viewer No. 1.

That was the role I played for most of my career. The guy on site looking around for the stories and then sending them home. For the most part, I kept a safe distance from my subject matter, but there was one dangerous, curvy ice queen I could not resist. I had to get up close and personal. Experience her myself. It got very personal. That snowy siren has left me broken and bruised—I have the X-rays to prove it—and still, even at age seventy-eight, I constantly crave her.

Ah, the Cresta! The first Lord Brabazon of Tara said, "The Cresta is like a woman with this cynical difference—to love her once is to love her always." I first fell for this exhilarating ice run in St. Moritz, Switzerland in 1967, while working as an associate director on ABC's coverage of the races. Producer Jim Spence felt that few in America would know of the Cresta Run, so he bestowed the title "The International Toboggan Championship," thinking it would be a better draw for the US audience.

To ride the Cresta is to dive headfirst onto a sled, called a skeleton, then drop 514 feet over three-quarters of a mile as you fly through ten turns that hug the rugged terrain, finally coming to a stop in the charming village of Celerina. Expert riders reach speeds of eighty miles per hour. After ABC's expert commentator for the Cresta, race car driver Sam Posey, took a run on the course in 1985, he said that he had never experienced a greater sensation of speed, not even in Grand Prix racing cars. He also said, "I now know what's it's like to be the front bumper of an automobile!"

The Cresta celebrated its 125th anniversary in 2010, and races have taken place every year since 1885, except for during the world wars. This natural ice run is rebuilt each year under the administration of the St. Moritz Tobogganing Club, which was formed by the British in 1885. Although it is a private club consisting of an international group of fun-loving people who span the social gamut from green grocer to royal, nonmembers are welcome to ride. Women are more restricted, however. Although they are welcomed members of the club, they were banned from the course in 1929 after a near-fatal crash. Still, women occasionally sneak on the course. *Wide World*'s cameras were there to cover such an occurrence in the 1980s. When the rider arrived at the finish, the helmet was removed and voilà! Long, beautiful blonde locks fell over the shoulders of a gorgeous woman. Since 2004, an official race has been held for the "weaker sex" on the last weekend of the season, but for the most part, the course is no-woman's-land, best exemplified by a sign high on the wall of the changing room in the clubhouse:

The St. Moritz Tobogganing Club
Where women cease from troubling and the wicked are at rest.

The Cresta Run is unique. The sport of skeleton also uses sleds, but they are built with more stealth, and races take place on slick, man-made bobsled courses. While bob runs have a concave design in an effort to contain riders within the tracks, the Cresta is deliberately shaped with shallower embankments. Consequently, a rider going too fast or out of control will fly out of the run. As the St. Moritz Tobogganing Club so matter-of-factly states on its website, "A curling stone sent down a bob run will arrive at the finish, a curling stone sent down the Cresta Run… will come out at the first such opportunity."

After watching rider after rider go down the run while we videotaped our television coverage in 1967, I wanted to feel the thrill myself. I also talked our production manager, Marvin Bader, into signing up. Today, beginners take a class, fondly referred to as The Death Talk. The highlight of this lecture, intended to make it clear that you are not about to ride the Matterhorn at Disneyland, is a full body X-ray pieced together from various accidents on the Cresta. The secretary points to certain broken bones, dislocated joints, fusion plates, and titanium rods, then identifies the club members to whom they belong. After the talk, beginners are instructed by a guru, an experienced club member who prepares you for the unforgettable descent.

In 1967, our preparation was a bit, shall I say, less formal. A club member simply put us on a skeleton with a sliding seat—which is a mis nomer because you don't sit on the seat, you lie on it—and told us to slide back and forth. We learned that shifting our body weight toward the back would add more pressure on the blades to dig into the ice. We also learned that the Cresta sleds have no steering mechanism. By changing hand positions, we would be able to keep the sled in the run—so we were told.

Caroming off ice at high speeds rips clothing—and skin—so we were issued protective gear. Many modern riders wear high-tech motocross protective gear to lessen the blow of those brutally bruising "Cresta kisses," but back in the day, we wore a helmet, elbow pads, kneepads, and steel gauntlets over our gloves (the latter are still in use today by beginners). We were also issued boots with a steel plate off the toe that had five sharp points, called a rake. The idea is to scrape the ice with these plates in an effort to help guide the skeleton and slow it down.

Although protective gear is required, it doesn't guarantee an injury-free journey. Fairchilds "Mac" Maccarthy, the illustrious American secretary of the club from 1949 to 1972, used to tell the story of a rider who took off his glove at the finish only to realize that the end of his forefinger was still inside! His hand had slipped under the runner as he negotiated Shuttlecock, Cresta's most infamous and aptly named turn.

During our coverage of the races, I learned all about Shuttlecock lore. There are basically two kinds of Cresta riders: those who left the run at Shuttlecock, and those who *will* leave the run at Shuttlecock. This ninety-degree sweeping left-hander is about two-fifths of the way down the course. It's intended to slow riders down, but about 80 percent of riders eventually crash there, landing in straw piled to cushion the blow. Anyone who exits the run at Shuttlecock becomes a member of "the most inexclusive club in the world"—the Shuttlecock Club. Members are entitled to wear the official Shuttlecock pin, tie, and suspenders (called "braces" by the British members).

Beginners start the course, minus the running start, about a third of the way down the course at a lower elevation called Junction; veterans start from the century-old octagonal building at the run's start called Top Hut. While Marvin and I waited our turn at Junction, C. K. (Keith) Williamson rode from Top. We heard three bells ring from the clubhouse tower, signaling there had been a fall. Keith had the misfortune to exit the course at the third turn, Thoma, a bad spot for a fall. Not many crash off the left side, so there is no straw. Keith went headfirst into a pipe that was sticking out of the surface of the snow and was badly injured. Riding stopped while he was attended to and the blood cleaned up that had stained the snowy embankment.

The news was unsettling to those of us suited up and ready to go at Junction. A fellow rookie rider took off his helmet and gloves and decided not to run. But I wasn't going to back down. I was going to ride the Cresta.

The clarion bell rang, signaling the rider ahead of me to move out of the start box. Then I heard my name echo through the valley, "Douglas Wilson, to the box."

Am I really going to do this? I thought as I lifted my toboggan into the hands of the arbeiter (attendant), stepped over the edge of the knee-high ice wall onto the run and into the start box…and waited…and waited.

"The next rider…Douglas Wilson!"

The clang of the bell jolted through me like a defibrillator shock. My heart was pounding; my breath was short. I was trying to remember what I had been told to do as I lay down on the sled. The arbeiter's foot was inches from my face, holding the toboggan in place. I stared down the icy trough, ready for whatever destiny had in store for me. The arbeiter's foot retreated from my line of vision. I lifted my feet, releasing the rakes, and the toboggan started to slide.

I picked up speed on Junction Straight, already feeling a little out of control. Posey was right. I had been watching riders for days on monitors in the TV truck, but to actually be four inches from the ice, face first, was a whole new perspective. I fought the instinct to rake right away, though I would soon discover that while one is approaching speeds of forty to sixty miles per hour, raking is as futile as trying to hold back a two-ton boulder on a forty-five-degree incline.

As instructed, I changed hand positions heading into Rise, a right-hander. I rose up the embankment but pulled her down, then whooshed under Nani's Bridge. Battledore came up quickly, a subtle right-hander. But no time to get cocky. Shuttlecock was next. I'd heard that the swash-buckling movie star Errol Flynn took the turn so slowly he stopped for champagne. Not I. I slid forward, as coached, and let her rip. Holy moly, Captain Marvel…It was like kicking in the afterburners. I "dived with a roar" through the open-ceilinged barrel of ice. The feeling of speed and lack of control was incomparable.

I was past Shuttlecock! You think you're safe, but there's no free ride to Finish. Three dangers still lurked ahead…Bulpetts…Scylla…and then a sharp right-hander named Charybdis. I dropped steeply and suddenly down into the final straightaway and crossed the finish line…But now you have to stop! The finishing banks are treacherous. You're like a run-away truck on one of those safety ramps on the highway. I slid to the left where I was finally stopped by spongelike mats and hay bales.

I've made it to Celerina! I couldn't stop giggling. The feeling reminded me of the first time I had sex. Scary, a little confusing, but I was eagerly looking forward to the next time!

I finished in 64.94 seconds, a typical time for a beginner. The fastest time that day was 47.78. I discarded caution and went for a second run and shaved 9.84 seconds off my time. Still determined, I went for a third and got my time down to 52.23.

Addicted, Marvin and I decided to stay another day. While en route to Junction in the camion before my fourth ride, a man named Gunter Sachs struck up a conversation. Gunter was a famous German industrial-ist, a Renaissance man with expertise in mathematics, photography, and astrology, among other disciplines, though he was best known at that time for being the husband of French movie star Brigitte Bardot. Gunter was also a sportsman. He was a longtime chairman of the St. Moritz Bobsleigh Club, and one of the turns on the track is named after him.

As we rattled along, Gunter inquired about my times. I told him I had just done a 52-second run. He said I was good, a natural.

"Really?" I blushed.

"Oh, yes," he said. "But you need a better toboggan. The one you have is no good. You would do better on a good toboggan. And don't rake."

I was convinced that I would make my mark as a great Cresta rider. When we arrived back at Junction, Gunter presented me with a fine toboggan, which weighed about twenty pounds more than the sixty pounder I had been riding. I can still hear his Germanic voice booming as I left the start: "Don't rake! Don't rake! Don't rake!"

I didn't. The ride was a totally new experience. I was no longer riding the Cresta—the skeleton was taking me for a ride. At Shuttlecock, I flew out like a pip from an orange, somersaulted twice in midair, and crashed into the straw. A few seconds after the sky stopped spinning, reality dawned on me. *I'm now a member of the most nonexclusive club in the world! I'm in the Shuttlecock Club!*

I've flown out of the course twenty times since then, but that was the only time I was happy about it. I rose to my feet and waved to the distant tower atop the clubhouse to signal that I was OK. Mac's voice blared on the PA system, "He's up and apparently unharmed!"

Upon returning to the clubhouse, I walked into a great celebration. As commentator Jack Whitaker said decades later, "Leaving the run at Shuttlecock is a matter of honor." Indeed. A Swiss member named Cha Cha Theler greeted me at the bar with champagne and the gift of a glass with the names of the Cresta turns etched on the side. He proudly draped a Shuttlecock tie around my neck and affixed a signature pin to my sweater. Later at lunch on the terrace of the Sunny Bar of the Kulm Hotel, he presented a typewritten letter verifying my accomplishment. He signed it as "The Life President of the Shuttlecock Club."

Forty years and over three hundred runs later, I was regaling the story to some members in the clubhouse. One of them told me that Gunter and Cha Cha used to bet on the success of beginners. A few days later I saw Cha Cha at a cocktail party.

"Cha Cha, I don't expect you would remember this, but in 1967, I went out at Shuttlecock. You bought me champagne, gave me a glass and a letter."

"I remember it well," he said.

"How much did you win?"

The tall, handsome Swede looked down at me with a devilish twinkle in his eye. "About a thousand francs."

9

Playing Politics

Nothing unites the people of the world like sports. This fact was always most evident at the Olympic Games, especially during the Closing Ceremony when the athletes from different countries abandoned all formalities and mingled their uniforms into a vibrant sea of color for one giant après-party. Then there was the more intimate expression of fellowship, such as when American decathlete Bill Toomey competed against his West German rival, Hans-Joachim Walde, at the Mexico City Summer Games in 1968. During the final event, the 1500 meters, Toomey crossed the finish line 1.4 seconds ahead of Walde to place sixth. Overall, Toomey took the gold medal, and Walde the silver. The two exhausted adversaries embraced one another. It was no different from when I saw Don Garlits's drag-racing team help a competitor get its vehicle ready in order to make it to the starting line on time.

We human beings are capable of incredible camaraderie, but just like countries, workplaces, neighborhoods, schools, families, and relationships, athletic competitions are not devoid of conflict and politics. I saw it all while I spanned the globe, whether it was about governmental philosophy, religion, race, gender, sexual orientation, steroids, scoring, or money. Most of the time, I saw sports help people celebrate the human spirit, but on occasion, idealism was trumped by pragmatism.

TECHNICAL FOUL

In 1969, I produced ABC's coverage of the World Gold Skate Classic—roller-skating, that is—held in the old Felt Forum at Madison Square Garden. This invitational competition was judged not only on technical ability but also on showmanship. The male World Roller Skating Champion, Michael Jacques, had a great act. Decked out as a magician in top hat, white gloves, and a black cape, Jacques made a grand entrance through an exploding cloud of smoke. Somehow, the director missed it. The officials realized we had missed the moment, and over a private phone line, offered to restart. I was delighted and grateful, and the second take worked fine.

About a week later, Roone stopped me in the office hallway. "Don't ever, ever stop a sports event again," he said sternly.

A few seconds passed before I understood what he was talking about. In defense, I told him that I did not motivate the restart, that the officials offered to do it.

"If you want to know any of the details," Roone said as he kept walking, "pick up a copy of *Newsweek*."

I was still befuddled.

"It just makes it a little difficult," Roone said, poking his head back around the corner, "when we've got Congress accusing television of controlling sports."

I made a beeline to the newsstand downstairs, and there it was on page ninety-eight: "Like a Houdini on roller skates, Michael Jacques glided into the arena…The 3,500 spectators…applauded wildly until they saw the television director from ABC dash onto the floor and yell frantically that Jacques would have to do it all again."

No wonder Roone was so angry—and it didn't matter that it wasn't *our* director who ran out onto the floor. Perception was reality. From 1951 to 1978, professional sports were evolving into big business, and over three hundred pieces of sports-related legislation were brought before the Senate and the House of Representatives. Roone was obviously aware that Congress was watching over the sporting world, including ABC, like a hawk.

Thankfully, on this and many other regrettably unforgettable occasions, Roone didn't fire me.

IRINA

During the depths of the Cold War, communications and aerospace technology enabled ABC Sports to fly over the Iron Curtain and send images of Eastern Europe and its people back to the States. Still, there remained a separation between "us" and "them." At international sporting events, Eastern athletes kept a safe distance from Western athletes and media. They were always aloof and stone-faced and rarely smiled. Sure, in an entertainment sport like figure skating, they were dramatic on the ice, but off it, *nyet*. Competitions were strictly business. They didn't seem to be having a good time in the way the American kids did. I came to understand this demeanor was part of the Eastern Bloc regimen. These athletes were trained to concentrate and intimidate.

When Soviet leader Mikhail Gorbachev instituted his "glasnost" policy in 1985, the Iron Curtain drew open further. The literal translation of the word is "openness," and a more relaxed atmosphere permitted freer access to information. As a result, we were able to get close enough to athletes and officials from the Communist nations to interact more personally with them. Truly get to know them.

In 1988, Dick Button hired retired Soviet skater Irina Rodnina to be a judge at the Challenge of the Champions in Paris. Dick, through his company Candid Productions, had created this competition for professional skaters as replacement programming when ABC lost the rights to televise the World Championships. Irina Rodnina was untouchable in pair skating in her day. She won ten consecutive World Pair Figure Skating Championships and three successive Olympic gold medals

(1972, 1976, and 1980). I covered almost all of these competitions for ABC and, despite the ability of a television camera to see everything in its range, was always frustrated by the barriers between the great Soviet champion and us.

Frustration was an understatement because Irina's skating history played like a prime-time soap opera, and it would have been great TV to have been able to interview her. First, there was the drama that unfolded at the 1972 World Championships in Calgary. Irina and partner Alexei Ulanov came into the competition fresh from their Olympic gold in Sapporo. The day before Worlds began, the two were practicing, and Irina fell out of a lift. She suffered a concussion and an intracranial hematoma. Still, she managed to make it through the short program despite residual pain and dizziness. As Irina came off the ice after their long program a couple of days later, she cried. They were clearly not tears of exhilaration and celebration, even though the performance earned them the top step of the podium. We assumed the sorrow was because Irina knew going into the competition, as did we and the rest of the media, that it would be the last time she would skate with Alexei. He had ended their partnership in order to skate with Lyudmila Smirnova, with whom he had fallen in love. As Irina collapsed in emotion, the Soviet team surrounded her, blocking our cameras from a clear shot. What a disappointment not to be able to get closer and perhaps hear what she might have been saying—even in Russian!

But the drama didn't end there. Irina considered retiring after the 1972 competition, but her coach suggested she try skating with Alexander Zaitsev. The next year at the World Championships in Czechoslovakia, Irina and her inexperienced partner made their first appearance on the world stage. Part way through their short program, the music stopped, but the two kept skating. It was one of the most uniquely dramatic moments I ever covered. Usually when there was a problem during a program, whether the wrong music was cued, the cassette tape broke, or a lace came untied, the skaters would stop and head over to the officials. They would then leave the ice to recompose, then start over or pick up where the music left off. But not Rodnina and Zaitsev. They soldiered on, despite the official at rink side waving them to stop. Even the ever-glib Dick Button was momentarily speechless! The sole sound of their blades cutting the silence in the arena was gripping. Toward the end, the crowd went nuts as they finished within one second of the actual music. Though Rodnina and Zaitsev had been skating together for less than a year, they took the World title. Smirnova and Ulanov finished second. Ulanov married Smirnova, Rodnina married Zaitsev, and her string of ten wins came to an end in 1979 when she gave birth to their first child. To no one's surprise, she was back in the saddle in 1980 to win one more Olympic gold at Lake Placid. This time, as she stood on the podium, the huge tear running down her cheek was a happy one.

In 1988, I was in Paris for the telecast of the Challenge of the Champions. The key broadcast personnel were set to dine together one evening, so I would finally be able to have a personal chat with Irina Rodnina. I even prepared for the get-together. Having worked globally for so many years, I wanted to do something about the political dynamics hindering people from a sense of world community. I had an idea. During my childhood in the early 1940s, the Soviet Union and America were allies, united against a common enemy, Nazi Germany. Why couldn't our two countries team again to fight a new common evil, such as cancer? Yes, we could go to war against cancer and save lives instead of destroying them!

We all met at Le Train Blue restaurant in the Gare de Bercy, the historic railroad station built in the early 1900s. I took a seat next to Irina in the grand room lit by chandeliers hanging beneath painted cathedral ceilings. To her right was Jirina Ribbens, a producer with Candid Productions, who was fluent in Russian and served as our interpreter. Irina spoke English but was naturally more comfortable expressing herself in her native language. Her demeanor was informal and friendly. I had always been intrigued by the depth of her very dark, mysterious eyes, which looked out from a girlish, pleasant face—not the face you'd expect on a tough, very tough, and dedicated competitor. We talked about many things, and finally, I asked her what really happened in 1973 when the music stopped. Irina told me she was so focused, so intent on victory, she just kept going, and Zaitsev followed her lead. Their decision makes more sense to me now than when I saw it happen because I learned over the years that skaters practice their routines more often without music than with it. They hear it in their heads. For many of them, the music is not the core, the pith of their programs. It is simply the veneer, the window dressing.

I was surprised to learn that Irina thought the tape had been sabotaged by a Czech dissident in protest of the Soviet oppression of the Prague Spring. This occurred in 1968, when Communist Czechoslovakia tried to democratize a bit, and the Soviet Union and other members of the Warsaw Pact, minus Romania, invaded the country in response.

I also asked Irina about her emotional breakdown when she came off the ice in Calgary in '72. She said two things evoked that reaction. One, she was relieved to have overcome her head injuries; second, she knew it was the end of her career with Ulanov. Her future was uncertain. The subject moved on to politics as Irina explained what it was like to go to America to compete in the late 1960s and '70s. She told me that a commissar had briefed the Soviet team members before embarking. They were given strict orders not to be friendly with anyone from the West, especially Americans. They were not to talk to anyone, unless approved by the Team Leaders. Do not form friendships. Do not give your address or phone number. Do not fraternize in any way. Irina further explained how angry she had become, amid the currently warming relations between the United States and the USSR, that the same commissar was now briefing the athletes to reach out, make friends, and form relationships with international fellow athletes! Irina told me that she had confronted this commissar and expressed her displeasure with what he had demanded of her and others in the past.

Irina then related to me how she was received when she returned to the Soviet Union from trips to America. She spoke of most everyone having cars, and supermarkets and shops that were abundant with goods. These common American pleasures were such a contrast to the store shelves in the Soviet Union, which were usually mostly bare. Irina told me that people had to stand in line for food. She found it infuriating to come home and talk about the wonders of the West, only to be told she had been taken to special places and seen a lie, propaganda created to show the United States to be something it was not. She knew what she had seen but had to appear to accept the party line.

At our dinner, Irina also told me that the changing attitudes at home in the USSR had a downside. It was very difficult for people like her father, who was a military man, to adjust. He had spent his entire career dedicated to hating the enemy, the United States, and trained for decades to fight against us. He felt his life had been wasted.

As dessert was served, I glanced around the gilded room that looked like a place where heads of state might meet and treaties would be signed. I then looked to Irina and proposed my American/Soviet War on Cancer. Perhaps together, she and I could motivate something out of the sports world that would benefit all humanity.

Irina smiled kindly, almost condescendingly. Then said in English, "That is a fine idea, but first…you must feed the people."

My music stopped.

With those simple words, Irina Rodnina gently turned this naive American away from reverie and toward reality.

ARTHUR

I arrived late for ABC's coverage of the 1990 Lipton Tennis Championships in Florida because I wanted to stay with my wife, Debbie, as long as possible. She had esophageal cancer. She was diagnosed with cancer of the larynx in 1988 and had a supraglottic laryngectomy procedure, but the cancer had metastasized to her esophagus and would later encroach further into her system. She had battled courageously, but medical science had no record of anyone in the world surviving inoperable esophageal cancer. So we knew, short of some kind of miracle, that the experimental chemotherapy she was receiving would eventually fail. Debbie was going to die.

I walked into the huge white tent that comprised the media center in Key Biscayne just as the preproduction meeting was about to begin. Crew members were jabbering, as usual, and starting to take seats on the folding chairs. Everyone knew why I had arrived at the last moment, and they were all very kind and supportive. Arthur Ashe, our expert commentator for the men's event, spotted me and quietly asked me to stay behind after the meeting. He wanted to talk to me about something.

After the tent emptied out, Arthur and I walked over to a corner in the back and sat down. I felt a bit strange. Arthur and I were colleagues, but not close friends. I had always admired him, not only for his tennis accomplishments and civil rights activism but also for the way in which he wore the mantle of champion. This was a man who grew up in the segregated South playing a traditionally white sport for the well-to-do; he went on to play professional tournaments held in clubs where he could not have even been a member at the time; and when he wanted to play in the 1969 South African Open, his visa was denied by that government due to its apartheid policy. Through it all, Arthur was the Gandhi of Tennis—quiet, unassuming, yet possessing a certain command of himself and those in his company. He motivated respect without ever asking for it and made history being the first—and to this day, only—African-American male to win the US Open (1968) and Wimbledon (1975).

In the corner of the empty VIP tent, Arthur Ashe looked me in the eye and said, "I am HIV positive. I have AIDS."

I was stunned.

He told me he had contracted the virus via a blood transfusion during one of his two heart bypass surgeries about ten years earlier. He then said he hated to burden me with his absolute secret, but he saw no other way to tell me that he had been thinking deeply about shortened life spans, and, knowing of my wife's situation, he wanted to share some writings he had been studying that might help me through this difficult time. He also told me that very few people knew of his illness and please to maintain his privacy.

To understand the risk that Arthur took, even as a heterosexual, sharing his secret with someone who worked in the media, is to understand the hostile societal attitude concerning AIDS and HIV during the 1980s. The AIDS virus was first detected in the United States in 1981, and there was a lot of fear surrounding the disease. Little was known about how it was transmitted, and funding for research was slow to start due to the paranoia over what was referred to then as "the gay disease." The epidemic was so controversial that the American government wouldn't begin an education campaign for another seven years. As a result, by

1995, AIDS was the number one cause of death among *all* Americans ages twenty-five to forty-four. Although contracting the HIV virus today isn't necessarily an impending death sentence, back then it was. Arthur Ashe, usually a very private man, disclosed his condition so he could console me, a business acquaintance, and trusted that I would keep his confidence. This touched me deeply.

I had already learned many times in life that there is only one way to keep a secret. That is to keep it. Do not tell anyone. I never told a soul, not even my wife. When Arthur and I met at events over the next two years, all I ever said to him in the casual way anyone would greet another was "Hi, Arthur. How are you?" He knew what I was really asking, and his simple reply told me he was all right. He was feeling OK.

When a national newspaper threatened to reveal that Arthur had AIDS in 1992, he decided it would be best to make the announcement himself. He did so in a press conference and, at week's end, was interviewed by Jim McKay on *Wide World of Sports*. As always, Arthur was gracious, and when he wrapped up his comments, he thanked ABC Sports, Jim, a couple of other people, then paused and mentioned me.

I had nothing to do with that interview. When colleagues asked me why he thanked me, I told them I had known about Arthur's illness for over two years. Arthur's "coming out" and activism, along with basketball superstar Magic Johnson's efforts (who had revealed he had HIV five months earlier), helped bring about compassion to those afflicted with AIDS as well as awareness and an urgency to fund research for a cure.

Debbie died in 1991. Arthur in early '93. That summer I took a trip to St. Moritz. With a sandwich and a small bottle of wine in a backpack, I hiked up to the start of the Cresta Run. There were no signs of the treacherous turns in sight, just gentle hillsides with grazing cows and meadows abounding with high grass and wildflowers reaching to the summer sun. I climbed over a split rail fence and worked my way down, finally reaching the area where the curves of Shuttlecock are carved with snow and ice in winter. With the glorious forces of life surrounding me, death was on my mind—the loss of a wonderful woman and a giant of a man.

At the spot where I had tempted my own mortality several times, I sat on a log and pulled out the only other item in my backpack, *Days of Grace*, the book Arthur had written shortly before he died. After finishing the final page, I paused to reflect on the advice Arthur gave to his daughter, Camera, in the last chapter, which was basically a manual to guide her into the twenty-first century since he would not be there with her. Arthur touched on every social and economic aspect of American life Camera would encounter. His closing words were: "[W]hen you stumble and fall and don't know if you can get up again, think of me. I will be watching and smiling and cheering you on."

And so I got up. With a renewed outlook. No longer thinking about death.

I meandered down the meadow, through the area of the winter finish line, and into the future.

BAD JUDGMENT

People often question whether sports like figure skating, gymnastics, and diving should even be considered sports because the competitors are judged. A "real" sport has a definitive winner determined by an absolute measure, such as baskets or runs, or being the first to cross or touch the finish line. No discussions, do doubts, no varying degrees of difficulty. Judging creates gray areas, and geopolitics clouds fairness even further.

Figure skating is the biggest culprit when it comes to scoring scandals. TV watchers in the new millennium may think that the players of CBS's *Survivor* invented alliances, but they were perfected decades before by the judges of the International Skating Union. I saw all kinds of collusion over the years, from the Eastern Bloc judges banding together against the West, to Europe as a whole voting against the United States, to France getting in bed with Russia. Prior to 1990, the competitors also had to earn the right—in the minds of the judges—to stand on the podium by working their way through the ranks. Before an American skater could compete at Nationals, he or she was expected to place in the top three at Juniors the year before and, before that, in the top three at Novice level. A new skater on the scene, whether national or international, had little chance of placing first, even if he or she clearly rose from the pack with a standout program in a competition. That sort of splash would be well noted for the future but would not achieve an immediate gold medal.

I saw this happen to Tim Wood in 1968, an Olympic year. At US Nationals (which were also the Olympic trials), all eyes were initially on the two men who had jockeyed back and forth for the American title the previous four years, Scott Allen and Gary Visconti. But when Tim, the defending bronze medalist, utterly commanded both the figures and the free skate, he was crowned the new US champion. Heading into the Winter Olympics in Grenoble, the judges' expectations were on the dueling Austrians, Emmerich Danzer (four-time World champion) and Wolfgang Schwarz. At the World Championships the previous two years, Danzer and Schwarz had finished one, two, followed by Visconti. At the Olympics, however, Visconti was out of the running for the gold, as far as the judges were concerned, because he had been dethroned by Tim Wood at US Nationals; and Tim wouldn't be a serious contender either because he had placed only ninth at Worlds the year before.

Danzer faltered badly enough in the Olympic compulsories to put him out of contention, no matter how well he would fare in the free skate. Meanwhile, Tim's very strong figures put him in second place, behind Schwarz. In the free skate, five judges placed Schwarz first and four placed Tim first. When the combined scores were tallied, Schwarz won the gold, Tim silver, and Frenchman Patrick Pera bronze. The Canadian judge then claimed he had made a mistake on his score sheet. He meant to place Tim first, which would have given Tim the Olympic gold. But the rules clearly stated that marks were not allowed to be changed. There was speculation at the time over the root of the so-called "clerical error," which renewed concerns of collusion in judging that wouldn't be confronted for another two decades. Nevertheless, the gold went to Schwarz. Three weeks later at Worlds, Danzer scored well enough in figures to regain favoritism...and the gold. The judges again placed Tim in second. The following year, with the two veterans having "retired" to the professional ranks, Tim could finally move into first place.

At the 2002 Winter Games in Salt Lake City, the fans sparked a revolution in judging during the pairs competition. NBC covered these Olympics, but I watched intently as I was still directing other figure skating events and competitions on ABC. Although the mostly North American crowd and the commentators clearly favored the hipper Canadian pair of Jamie Salé and David Pelletier, the gold went in a controversial decision to the more traditional Russian team of Yelena Berezhnaya and Anton Sikharulidze. There was outcry in the stadium, on the air, and in the press. That night, the French judge admitted to having struck a deal with the Russians. In an unprecedented move, another gold was awarded to the Canadians.

Under pressure to make its judging less partial—or at least appear to be—the ISU overhauled its scoring system. Several proposals were made, including one by the US Figure Skating Association, which essentially kept the 6.0 system, threw out the two highest and lowest marks, and averaged the remaining five. This is the system that should have been adopted because the "Code of Points" system that took effect in 2005 has done nothing but make the sport less appealing to watch and has contributed significantly to its decline.

First of all, the new system is so complex the crowd can no longer decipher a score. Gone is the fun of a string of scores flashing across the board and the crowd booing or cheering as each judge's number is called out by the announcer: "Five point eight, five point nine, five point nine…" Today, only one total score is posted. People understood a perfect 6.0. There is no perfect score anymore, and a winning total lands somewhere around 200 points, give or take 50-something. The new system may have more judges and "technical specialists," but their individual nationalities are hidden from the public, which seems to undermine the goals of honesty and integrity. These cloaked calculations have also robbed the fans the pleasure of booing a judge with whom they don't agree. But most importantly, the artistic presentation score, which used to account for *half* the score in a free skate, has been drastically diminished. The score became nearly all technical, which has caused skaters to load their programs with maneuvers that will earn them more points. Also, so many minor elements are now required that individual creativity has been stifled. The result? Figure skating, which used to be the hot ticket at the Winter Olympics, has lost so much popularity that they now have to give away tickets to fill the seats! Same at the World Championships. Corporate sponsors have backed out. US Figure Skating's annual budget has taken a 30 percent dive from its high in 1998—the sport just isn't as appealing since ditching the 6.0 system.

Even though the scoring changes were made with good intentions—to eliminate bias and politics from a so-called "artistic" sport—figure skating has suffered. Less interpretation of the music means that the skaters connect less with the audience. They have become "point junkies," as Tim said in a recent conversation. He also said, "You used to know what a Janet Lynn looked like on the ice, or a Peggy Fleming or a Dorothy Hamill. They each had a unique style." Today it's all about the "arithmetricks."

Has figure skating become too much of a "real" sport?

I recently watched Peggy Fleming's 1968 gold medal performance on YouTube and noticed a post made by Joe Williams, writing as Twisterjoe, in 2010. His comments say it all:

> All you who are not impressed that she does not do as many turns or jumps as today, PLEASE LOOK AT THE BEAUTY. THE PHRASING, THE GRACEFUL SINCERITY. A lot of this is not just about what she can do, but what an artist can make you feel...

BROAD CASTING

I am often asked what I think have been the most significant developments in the evolution of sports television production since its golden age. Jet travel made the world more easily accessible, and Telstar, the first satellite, provided a twenty-minute pocket of time during which a television signal from Europe could be seen in North America...live! Early Bird then ushered in the era of fixed satellites that shrank our vast planet into a multicultural village 24/7. Videotape enabled editing; handheld and underwater cameras gave us new points of view; and replays and slow motion brought even more texture to our broadcasts. Two-inch videotape morphed into one-inch, resulting in faster rewind capability, and graphics gave rise to visual sophistication. It's hard to believe now that we first used deli menu boards for graphics, inserting white plastic letters into the slots on a black, felt-like board that was superimposed on the screen! (During one NBA telecast, Oscar Robertson became "Big O" for the afternoon when I ran out of *R*s!) Videotape then gave way to digitized information. Now we've got wide-screen TVs with life-size pictures in high-definition that make even the commercial bumpers from a blimp's-eye view worth watching.

But that was all technical stuff.

There was one human element that was introduced to ABC Sports in the 1970s that turned *everything* upside down and monumentally changed how we worked and what we televised:

WOMEN!

One June 23, 1972, President Richard Nixon signed Title IX into law, which stated that "No person in the US shall, on the basis of sex be excluded from participation in, or denied the benefits of, or be subjected to discrimination under any educational program or activity receiving federal aid." This legislation applied to both academics *and* athletics and reverberated throughout American society in general, including the workplace. Changes were particularly evident at ABC Sports where there had previously been no women on our crews, and few women's sports were covered because there simply weren't many then beyond gymnastics, swimming, figure skating, and alpine ski racing.

I will never forget waiting for an elevator with Eleanor Sanger Riger on the twenty-eighth floor at corporate headquarters. Eleanor had the distinction of being the first female network sports producer when she was hired at ABC in 1973. While we waited, Eleanor gazed up at the huge collage of sports photos on the wall and pointed out that the only female athlete in it was a horse! That lone female was Genuine Risk, winner of the 1980 Kentucky Derby.

When the stadium gates opened for female athletes in the 1970s, out burst tennis champion Billie Jean King. On September 20, 1973, I was a spectator at the Houston Astrodome for ABC's prime-time telecast of "The Battle of the Sexes," a mega-hyped tennis match between two Wimbledon champions: twenty-nine-year-old King and fifty-five-year-old Bobby Riggs. King was the model representative for her gender.

She ruled Wimbledon, having already won seventeen of her soon-to-be record twenty titles there, yet she did not receive the same prize money as the men (this wouldn't change until 2007). She, like other female players, was also identified as either "Miss" or "Mrs." on the scoreboards (which would continue until 2009). On the other side of the court was Riggs, who willingly cast himself as the villain and maintained that women didn't deserve equal prize money. Already known for being a hustler and an opportunist, Riggs milked his male-chauvinist-pig gig for all it was worth. On game day, he entered the stadium donning a Sugar Daddy jacket (sponsored by the candy maker) and perched atop a rickshaw pulled by six gorgeous women. But King upstaged him, arriving in a gold litter held aloft by six bare-chested hunks. She also cradled an adorable little pig, which she presented to Riggs. Over thirty thousand spectators and fifty million people watching worldwide made the spectacle the largest live telecast of a tennis match ever. King won 6–4, 6–3, 6–3 in a contest the *London Times* described as "the drop shot and volley heard round the world."

If King had been playing a man her own age, like Jimmy Connors, the result most likely would have been different. Men are physically stronger by nature. Still, King had to have incredible emotional resolve to withstand the pressure on her that day. King did way more than mute a loud-mouthed carpetbagger who mocked and derided female athletes. She ignited the women's movement. Her presence and accomplishments during that decade, which included founding the Women's Tennis Association and fighting for equal prize money, enabled women everywhere to feel comfortable about being active, playing sports, speaking up, and becoming a doctor instead of a nurse or a pilot instead of a stewardess. Billie Jean King became the face of women's liberation, whether she intended to or not. There could not have been a more perfect poster ~~girl~~ woman.

The long, gradual movement toward equality—the Nineteenth Amendment, Rosie the Riveter, The Pill, Title IX—empowered and energized women, and Billie Jean King and that certain tennis match on September 20, 1973, cannot be separated from that progression. But the King/Riggs match also reflected the tension between the sexes at the time. While my sons, ages fourteen, twelve, and seven, rooted for King, I privately rooted for Riggs—and suspected that most men did, too—but didn't want to admit it. I was torn between supporting equal rights for women and giving up the stature, power, and assumed authority I enjoyed in what had previously been a man's world. My mates and I didn't want our privileges diminished, and we were starting to get defensive.

Before any woman reading this wants to turn me into bacon, please let me explain. People still refer to the business world as "the boys' club," and back in the 1970s, the business of television sports was the mother of all boys' clubs, an eternal locker room. Enter women: on camera and behind it, and, admittedly, my colleagues and I had some difficulty adjusting to the changes. One reason was it seemed that men were made out to be bad just because we were men. If I opened the door for a woman, I was insulting her. If I took my hat off in an elevator that I shared with a woman, I was offending her. I just didn't understand—my mother and father taught me to do such things out of respect, not condescension. My mother also taught me that it was a man's duty to protect a woman, such as taking the outside position on a sidewalk.

Then came the company meetings on harassment in the workplace, and the subject was always about a man doing something wrong to a woman, such as speaking harshly or using foul language. Though it wasn't said, the message was clear: making sexual advances was absolutely verboten, and any physical contact, even touching a shoulder, would be cause for suspension or dismissal.

We men had never pussyfooted around each other. Many producers and directors would curse at their colleagues, grab collars, or yell at underlings to just get the damned job done! Macho behavior didn't matter when it was all men. But in a coed workplace, we could no longer focus *solely* on the job. During the chaos of a control room countdown to air, having to think about *how* we talked to someone was initially a huge and unwelcomed distraction.

When I was directing additional footage for a Boitano/Witt feature on *Wide World*, we were set up on the ice for an interview of the two skaters by my coproducer, "Maxine," and another up-and-coming producer, Kathy Cook. I walked over to make a suggestion, and Maxine said, loudly enough so the entire crew and onlookers could hear, "This is none of your business, Doug. This is Kathy's show!" I was outraged. I wanted to take hold of the back of her chair, yank it across the ice away from everyone, pull her up by the collar of her full-length mink coat, and tell her to never, *ever*, talk to me like that in public again. If Maxine had been a Max, I might have even decked him. But Maxine was not a Max, so I took a deep breath and calmly said, "I don't believe Brian would agree with you," and walked away.

For the record, I did punch a male colleague once. Right in the stomach. I regretted it afterward, but I did do it. However, to be in the same situation opposite a woman is like being a high school wrestler who finds out his opponent is a girl. I know she joins the boys' team because there is no other option, but the setup itself has inherent flaws. Any guy who competes against the girl is between a rock and a soft place! Every move, every grab contradicts what the boy has been raised to believe is inappropriate contact with the opposite sex. Throwing a girl down to the mat with a crotch lift and then pinning her with a crossface cradle just isn't right. If he wins, he's a bully beating a girl. If he loses, he'll never hear the end of it!

That is why I rooted for Bobby Riggs.

Nevertheless, we men had to learn quickly that a woman at work was to be considered a colleague. Not a female colleague, simply a colleague, gender neutral. We were to interact with a woman in a way that was appropriate. We were not to acknowledge a woman's attractiveness or how she dressed or behaved, even if she *seemed* to be inviting attention.

Men weren't the only ones perturbed about changes in the workplace. I knew one woman who had worked her way up to general manager at a television station. She came out of a harassment meeting at her company and was livid. She told me she had worked her entire career to be treated like "one of the boys"—to zero in on her goals and go after them. She didn't want people to tiptoe around her or worry about her "feelings." She could sling profanities like hash and was deeply irritated that she would no longer be treated the same way as her male colleagues.

On the other hand, such changes in the workplace allowed men to see that we definitely went too far at times. I recall one episode that involved preeminent producer Chet Forte. Although Chet deserved all of the accolades he received during his career, he could be a real tyrant. He often degraded subordinates over the headsets. One such victim was a sharp, young production assistant in the early 1970s whom I'll call "Doris." During a *Monday Night Football* telecast, she goofed on a graphic, and Chet screamed into his headset, "Doris, you cocksucker!" This dubious moniker stuck with Doris during her tenure at ABC Sports. It was not unusual for someone to say, "Hi, D-U-C-S" if he crossed her path—and she would respond civilly. Now the previously mentioned female executive might say it was a compliment to Doris in that she was being treated just like everyone else—and this was true. Chet would have said the same words to a man. To Doris's credit, she "took it like a man" and never displayed any bitterness or anger about the incident—at least not at the workplace.

I suppose I have to blame my attitudes partially on my unconventional mother, who, beyond the advantages of wealth, had the guts to pursue activities and goals usually reserved for men. Frances Louise Seydel was one of only three women in the graduating class of 1929 at the University of Michigan to receive a doctorate—in astronomy, no less, with an emphasis in physics. She played a fine game of tennis, rode horseback astride the animal, and was the only female in the pack when she went hunting with her father and his cronies in northern Canada. In a time when young women didn't travel alone, my mother and her best friend toured Europe. She skied in St. Moritz in bear trap bindings—packing a lunch to make the climb by foot—and left a trail of bleeding men's hearts as she and her friend sashayed through England, Spain, and Central Europe. Over lunch in 1979, I asked my mother what she thought about the revolutionary women's movement of the past ten years. The lovely, silver-haired lady looked across the table and said matter-of-factly, "Well, I don't really understand it. I always did whatever I wanted to do."

Despite my upbringing and some of my opinions, I came to understand what it was like for those female pioneers in sports television to be the only woman on a crew when I was the lone man on a broadcast. Sitting at dinner with a group of women, I felt like I was observing a private gathering. They weren't consciously excluding me. It was just a natural thing for the "girls" to chat and laugh with each other. Over time, I also realized that the work environment was tougher for women because they were judged differently. I recall inviting a young, female production assistant to sit in the producer's chair at a ski jumping event. She put on the headset, and the lovely, soft-spoken woman turned into a monster!

She shouted orders in a demeaning manner in the mold of the worst of her predecessors. I was shocked. For years I had worked with men who did the same and never said a word, even though I felt such conduct was neither constructive nor productive. I confess I am no better than a tennis fan who thought Ilie "Nasty" Nastase's and John McEnroe's bad-boy antics on court during the 1970s and '80s were as entertaining as they were deplorable, but I was absolutely appalled when Serena Williams threatened a line judge and badgered an umpire.

And how can we talk about women in sports broadcasting without discussing whether or not women should be allowed in men's locker rooms? Especially in this era of instant communications, a female reporter is at a disadvantage if she can't go into the locker room after a game. I gave a lecture at Ithaca College when this issue was in the headlines. One of the coeds asked what I thought about it. I told her that I thought it was justified. Then, for the sake of show, I said, "As long as I can go into the women's locker room."

Well, she hadn't thought about that! Neither had any of the other students in the room. But they did think that the idea of my entering a women's locker room was unacceptable. Technically speaking, it should be no different, but there are double standards that go both ways. I was waiting for a female colleague when she emerged from the men's locker room after a professional soccer game, and the first thing out of her mouth was how delicious looking all the men's butts were! Years later, while working on the "Canvas of Ice" special, Amy Sacks Feld, my coproducer, chatted with the costumer at rink side. The bulk of their conversation centered around how to dress Brian to exploit his powerful thighs and calves, not to mention his great ass. After eavesdropping for a few minutes, I approached the two and commented that if I had said those same things about Katarina Witt, I would be criticized for inappropriate behavior and possibly reprimanded, and any woman within earshot would think I was a jerk.

Interestingly, as the years passed, I generally preferred to work with women over men. They did their jobs with a level of detail and devotion that made them indispensable. For example, while watching skaters rehearse at rink side, I'd call out camera shots to my assistant, who wrote them down and marked time with a stopwatch. During the telecast, my assistant would tell me via headset which camera I had chosen as each moment approached. My male assistants always used the notes they had prepared at rehearsals. The women, however, generated a new list for my needs and a second for theirs that utilized a color-coded system, diagrams showing the skater's position on the ice, the direction their body faced, and the direction their head faced. The men did what was necessary; the women went above and beyond.

This whole gender issue was, and remains, a touchy, complex subject, with fine lines where both sides can be effectively argued. In the end, however, it's a good thing that women joined the workforce at ABC and that we started to cover more female athletic events—and that there are now more female events to cover! The sexes will always battle, but as the title of Billie Jean King's book about the history of women's tennis states, "We have come a long way."

As far as my personal evolution, I've been the recipient of a number of honors during my career, but I thank Kathy Cook for the one that would make my mother especially proud. During the making of a skating special that Kathy produced and I directed, Kathy made me "An Honorary Woman."

10

Still Rings

Jim McKay aptly referred to the Olympic Games as a town meeting of the world. In 1972, that town meeting was held in Munich, West Germany. ABC Sports had been preparing for years, including conducting new levels of research into the athletes' backgrounds for the debut of our soon-to-be-famous "Up Close and Personal" profiles. We would also be using more handheld cameras than we did in Mexico City in '68 and taking advantage of geosynchronous satellites that would give us the ability to make continuous live television transmissions. This technical ability was significant because we would be broadcasting from a different hemisphere, and it is also what made our nonstop live coverage of the impending crisis possible.

The 1970s were our halcyon days at ABC. *Wide World* had celebrated its tenth anniversary in '71, and Roone's office shelves were filled with Emmys. Decked out in swag—shirts, jackets, and other assorted goodies emblazoned with the ABC Sports Olympic patch—the crew headed to JFK International. Like all air travelers in those days, we simply checked our luggage and walked straight through the terminal to the gate and onto the plane. We were all eager and excited to get to Munich to hear those classic words, "Let the Games begin!"

As our plane approached Munich, I thought about the first time I had flown into the city, which was eight years earlier on my way to the

1964 Winter Olympics in Innsbruck. The man sitting next to me, who had fought in World War II, reminded me that the Munich airfield was once the site of Luftwaffe Headquarters. The Luftwaffe was the powerful German air force that supported Hitler's *blitzkrieg*, literally "lightning war," across Europe. I couldn't help but think about all the radio shows I listened to as a kid, especially the ones about the ace pilots, *Hop Harrigan,* who was "America's Ace of the Airwaves," and *Captain Midnight.* These programs implanted in my youthful mind a palpable fear of the enemy. Now I was landing at their headquarters! I looked at the buildings through the eyes of my boyhood. Pockmarks still etched the walls from Allied shelling. As we entered the terminal, my fellow passenger remarked that the last time he had entered the space, ammunition crates were packed from floor to ceiling. I truly felt scared.

The first German I encountered was a customs officer in a uniform that I had always envisioned on a Gestapo officer—dark gray with a high-brimmed military-style cap. I fully expected to see a swastika above the brim or somewhere in the room. I couldn't understand any signage until I finally spotted one that said "*Trink Coca Cola.*" The sight of that great American trademark relaxed me a little and reminded me it was 1964, not 1945.

In 1972, much of Europe still had a militaristic, post-war feel to it. The Iron Curtain was still standing strong, and it would be another seventeen years before the Berlin Wall would fall, reuniting Germany. It would be another two years after that before the Soviet Union would collapse. Although awareness of Muslim extremism and Arab terrorism was hardly known or understood by the general public in Western nations at the time, the memories of Nazi Germany still lingered.

The West Germans, who landed on the free side of divided, post-war Germany, were keenly aware of this sensitivity. They wanted to set a tone completely opposite of the very militaristic one set in 1936, when Chancellor Adolph Hitler used the Berlin Summer Games as a world stage to showcase the supremacy of his "Master Race." For the Munich Games, the West Germans were dedicated to creating an atmosphere of peace, tranquility, and healthy competition in hope of recasting themselves and their country in the eyes of the world. Their official symbol was a bold, graphic sun design representing light, freshness, and generosity. Their official mascot was Waldi, a harmless multicolored dachshund (minus the National Socialist Party colors of black and red)—a breed with an image that couldn't be more opposite of the German shepherd, Hitler's canine preference. Their official motto was "The Happy Games," and the Dove of Peace was seen on posters throughout the city. They built a striking, avant-garde stadium with a tentlike canopy made of sweeping steel cables and panels of acrylic glass. This airborne transparency evoked not only the nearby Alps but also the "new" Germany. Great swaths of fabric in soft pastels of blue, yellow, and green were hung from streetlight poles and municipal buildings. They even dressed the police in pastel blue shirts.

Our pre-Olympic telecast the night before the Opening Ceremony played on the peace theme, too. It included a video that ABC News foreign correspondent Peter Jennings and I had put together about the history of the Olympic site in Munich (Roone had borrowed Peter from the News Department for the Games). The land set aside for the 1972 Olympic Park was notable for two things: the Munich Agreement and a large hill made from the rubble left after the Allied bombing raids. In 1938, Hitler gathered Britain's Neville Chamberlain, France's Edouard Daladier, and Italy's Benito Mussolini to sign the Munich Agreement. In this agreement, the powers of Europe agreed to allow Germany to annex Czechoslovakia's Sudetenland in exchange for peace. Chamberlain returned home and was well received with his "Peace in our time" speech. Not even a year later, Germany invaded Poland, and World War II began. Seventy percent of Munich lay in ruins after the war. To clean up the city, the rubble was gathered and dumped in two places, one of them forming the giant heap now known as Olympiaberg. Over time, this 50-meter-high, 1300-meter-wide hill became a park. During the video feature, Peter told us that the Germans built the hill "to remind themselves, and remind other people who see it, simply how futile war really is. So now it is an Olympic hill, and down below for the next two weeks there's going to be that great international attempt to be one in brotherhood athletically."

Peter then narrated more historical facts over black-and-white "B-roll" of the four European leaders signing the treaty. The song we used was Burt Bacharach and Hal David's 1965 inspirational hit, "What the World Needs Now is Love." One cut showed the victory arch Siegestor, circa 1945, which had been heavily damaged during the war. This monument, commissioned by King Ludwig I of Bavaria to commemorate his army's victory during the Napoleonic Wars, was only partially restored in the 1950s so that it also stood as a symbol of peace. As the song's key rose to an even more exhilarating level, the black-and-white images of the archway dissolved into the restored gate in 1972 in full color. Modern-day Munich was now a happy, peaceful city, filled with joy for the upcoming Games and Bavarian *Gemültichkeit* (friendship and goodwill). Peter closed with, "On the eve of these Games, athletes from all over the world are here now in the Olympic Village. And although there have been political crises in the last week"—he was referring to Rhodesia having been barred from the Games for its apartheid policies—"now it doesn't seem to matter where they come from on an individual basis. They're here to meet, to admire, and have a cup of tea, and make friends."

For ten days, the Munich Games would, indeed, show the world a new vision of Germany. My assignment the first week was a gem: producing and directing the gymnastics coverage in the newly built Olympiahalle, right next to the Olympic Stadium. Gymnastics is a very challenging sport to cover because during the team and all-around competitions, four or six events are going on simultaneously. I felt some added stress in that I would not have the usual technical director on hand. So, while my producer eyes would be surveying several monitors for the stories that had been discussed in production meetings, as well as spotting any worthy new developments, my brain would be choosing which camera angle to air, and my hands would be sliding levers and pushing buttons on the console! I would also have to learn how to operate unfamiliar equipment. Thankfully a German technician named Hans helped me out.

Gymnastics did not enjoy much popularity in the United States until Cathy Rigby came along. She was the first American woman to win an international medal in the sport when she took the silver in balance beam at the 1970 World Championships. Her elfin-like personality and stature endeared her to fans. The Munich Games would be Rigby's second Olympics, and we planned to highlight her in our coverage. Unfortunately, Rigby's overall performance wasn't up to her usual caliber. She also purposefully left an aerial out of her beam routine in order to secure a team bronze in case anything went wrong with that risky move. An honorable sacrifice for the team, but in the end, Rigby didn't qualify for the individual final in her specialty, the balance beam, and the US team finished fourth.

The big drama that unfolded in gymnastics and spiked the ratings turned out to be another pigtailed petite blonde…from the Soviet Union. On our first day of gymnastics coverage, Olga Korbut, the seventeen-year-old newcomer, contributed to the Soviet team gold with a standout performance on the uneven parallel bars. The crowd loved her, as did our television cameras. Her routine was gutsy and flawless from the start and included a soaring back summersault off the upper bar—the first backward release ever on the apparatus—followed by a backward flip around the lower bar that catapulted her back up to the high bar, which she blindly grabbed with both hands.

"Has that been done before by a girl?" Jim asked our expert commentator Gordon Maddux.

"Never. Never!" Maddux exclaimed. "Not by any human that I know of!"

When Korbut stuck her landing after another blind leap in her dismount from the upper bar, she received an "Oh my, wow!" from Maddux, but only a 9.8 from the judges. The crowd vehemently protested the "low" mark. That performance, coupled with contortionist-like moves on the balance beam, made Olga Korbut a household name across the United States overnight. Every little girl in America wanted to become a gymnast.

Korbut's splashy debut sparked an unexpected intra-team rivalry on the powerful Soviet squad. Lyudmila Turishcheva came into the Munich Games as the leading lady of the Soviet team and the grand dame of international women's gymnastics, which she had completely dominated since 1970. But the taller, elegant, long-legged champion was outshined by her shorter, younger, pluckier teammate. Female Soviet gymnasts tended to be like Turishcheva, made from the classic, Russian ballerina mold: graceful, elegant, composed, and controlled. Korbut was, well, more American-like! For the same reasons people liked Cathy Rigby, they liked Olga Korbut. She wore her emotions on her sleeve and acknowledged the crowd directly with her broad smile and waving hands. She expressed joy. This was unusual behavior for an Eastern Bloc athlete, and Korbut was also incredibly talented…not to mention telegenic. The tension between the two Soviets made for great television, as Korbut not only stole the spotlight from Turishcheva but also a few medals. And to think that the four-feet-eleven-inch, ninety-pound, pigtailed Belorussian was a mere alternate who got called up to the squad when another teammate got injured!

In the all-around competition, we watched Korbut run for the gold after solid finishes in the vault and floor exercise. Then, to our disbelief, she totally choked in her specialty, the uneven bars. She was off from the start, stubbing her toes on her mount and later again in the routine. The bubble burst in the arena, back at the ABC Broadcast Center, and around the world. Korbut completed her routine, then broke into tears on the team bench. Once again, our cameras caught it all, and Korbut didn't hold back. Turishcheva took the all-around gold, but the next day, Korbut made a terrific comeback on the uneven bars to win the silver, then took gold on the balance beam and edged out Turishcheva for the gold in her forte, the floor exercise.

When we concluded our gymnastics coverage with the men's individual apparatus events two days later, we were riding high at ABC. As our gymnastics crew would be dispersing to different venues for the remainder of the Games, we gathered outside the mobile van for a brief celebration. We toasted each other for a job well done, proud to have raised awareness of gymnastics in the United States. We also talked about how lucky we were to be involved in this television adventure.

"Hmmmm, champagne in paper cups," remarked Donna Maddux, Gordon's wife.

I raised my cup to my German TV brother-in-the-bond, to whom I was deeply indebted for his guidance and teaching me how to use the equipment. "Hans," I said, "if we had been standing here twenty-seven years ago, we wouldn't be drinking champagne. We would be trying to kill each other, and isn't that ridiculous!"

"Yah," he responded with a smile.

We shook hands and embraced. *What the world needs now…*

I looked up at the sky and noticed that the beautiful weather we had been enjoying all week was starting to change.

I moved on to boxing, which wasn't nearly as exciting as gymnastics had been because many of the matches were lackluster—so lackluster that I struggled with my recommendations to Roone about which fights to air. The one bout that everyone thought would deliver high ratings was the Bobick/Stevenson heavyweight quarterfinal on Tuesday, September 5. About nine o'clock that morning, I awoke in my room on the seventeenth floor of the Munich Sheraton and looked out over the city. Strange… there were two tanks on the avenue below. They seemed so out of place, so discordant against the memories of the past week. I assumed there was going to be some sort of parade that day.

I turned on the TV and was shocked to see a news anchor reporting a grim situation in the Olympic Village. Apparently, hostages had been taken. Security was minimal in those days. All you needed to enter the village and mingle with the athletes were the proper credentials. I had to get to the Broadcast Center, to the center of things. During the fifteen-minute ride, I gazed up at the pastel banners and doves of peace adorning the broad avenue and felt such anger. I was born in 1935, and there were no Olympic Games when I was a kid. They were suspended after the 1936 Games in Berlin due to World War II, and they would not resume until 1948. So, at age thirteen, to see the countries of the world come together for sport, not war, was momentous. And that they took place in London, where there was still rubble in the streets from the German air raids, made my first Olympics even more meaningful. At thirty-seven, as I walked into the Broadcast Center and gazed in the direction of the Olympic Village, I hadn't lost my awe for the Games or my belief in the Olympic ideal. It wasn't religion, but it was damned close. So to think about what was going on beyond that fence was sacrilege.

Once inside, Jim McKay was already on the air. It was supposed to have been his day off. He had taken a swim and was in the hotel sauna when he got the message from ABC's coordinating producer for the Games, Geoffrey Mason. Sixteen hours later, Jim's bathing suit would still be damp under the trousers he had hurriedly pulled on in his rush to handle the live coverage of the unfolding emergency.

Instead of broadcasting Olympic events, our focus now turned to 31 Connollystrasse, where a group of Palestinian terrorists, who called themselves Black September, were holding eleven hostages, all of them members of the Israeli delegation. The terrorists had jumped a fence to gain access to the village after 4:00 a.m. They had already killed two Israelis, a wrestling coach and a referee, and had dumped the coach's naked body onto the street to demonstrate they were to be taken seriously.

Media from around the globe gathered like a mob, all our cameras searing images into the memories of viewers worldwide, most notably of one terrorist who ventured out onto the balcony, his face hidden under a socklike mask. The odd thing was, Olympic competition was still in progress, and I had a job to do. That's how crazy things were. I had to get to a cubical to record the feed of the boxing matches in process, then screen the video for editing and presentation. Stevenson destroyed Bobick in the third round, but the fight seemed so unimportant to me, not just because it was a total disappointment but because we were all distracted by the hostage situation.

Along with my colleagues, I helped in whatever way I could in the studio, the tape room, and the control room. Roone commanded operations, sitting beside director Don Ohlmeyer at the TV console continuously. Roone needed to be certain that all facts had been verified before going on the air, and there was so much confusion. Senior Production Manager Marvin Bader was on the phone all day trying to gather information from both government and Olympic officials. Another colleague, John Wilcox, disguised himself as an athlete and managed to sneak into a room in a building across from, but very close to, the center of the crisis in the Olympic Village.

Our coverage was continuous, with the exception of one short break, when CBS took control of the satellite, having previously booked it for its daily updates. ABC had the complete rights to the Munich Games for the United States, so Roone kept the crisis coverage exclusive on ABC. In 1972, there were only a handful of channels, and news was broadcast only a couple of times a day. ABC Sports suddenly became a round-the-clock news organization. It was a natural fit for all of us, especially for

Jim, whose journalism roots were planted at *The Baltimore Sun*, where he had been a reporter. He was a newsman at heart. That day, he was ABC's Walter Cronkite. Peter Jennings's contributions were also invaluable. Of course, when Roone brought Peter on board the Olympic broadcast team, he had no idea how relevant his expertise on the Middle East would become.

Early that morning, the terrorists dropped a list of demands out the window. They wanted the release of 234 Palestinians and non-Arabs jailed in Israel, and two German radicals held in West Germany, and they wanted them all safely transported to Egypt. Deadlines kept being pushed back, but Israel would not negotiate. The country did offer to send a special forces unit to Germany, but Chancellor Willy Brandt refused. The whole thing was bizarre. One moment our cameras showed terrorists peeking out windows, German authorities negotiating with the terrorists, and sharpshooters positioning themselves on nearby rooftops; then the tower camera would pan over to another area of the Olympic Village where athletes were sunbathing and playing Ping-Pong. Competitions were still going on, too!

At 4:00 p.m., Avery Brundage, president of the IOC, finally suspended competition. I took a break to get some air and walked over to the fence that surrounded the Olympic Village. I stood there and stared...31 Connollystrasse was only about one hundred yards away. It was hard to fathom what was going on inside.

At 5:00 p.m., another deadline passed. With negotiations going nowhere, the terrorists demanded air transport for them and the hostages to Cairo. The West Germans agreed but were actually planning to storm the apartment. Unfortunately, the terrorists became aware of the plan. We learned more about this when West German police carrying heavy weapons entered our control room. They didn't speak English but were able to vehemently communicate that we were to cease airing images from the tower camera because there were television sets in each room in the village, and it was suspected that the terrorists were watching our broadcast along with everyone else. Roone cooperated, of course, but after they left he recorded the tower view so we could play it back later.

Around 10:30 p.m., the kidnappers and their hostages were transferred first by bus, then by helicopter to a military airport. As the buses pulled away, I felt optimistic that the situation was under control, as I think we all did. Today, an Aristotle quote my high school social studies teacher had displayed in his classroom comes to mind: "The greatest obstacle to clear thinking is that people tend to believe what they want to believe."

But soon, as Jim McKay later reported on the air, "All hell broke loose." The West German police disguised as flight crew aboard the waiting Boeing 727 abandoned their mission and didn't tell anyone. When a couple of the terrorists boarded the waiting plane and realized they were being ambushed, all hell did, indeed, break loose. Under gunfire, one of the terrorists shot four hostages tied to their seats in one of the helicopters, then threw in a grenade. Another terrorist killed the remaining hostages in the second helicopter with his machine gun.

In the early hours of September 6, I stood beside one of the studio cameras and watched as Jim discussed the situation with Peter Jennings, Bonn News Bureau Chief Lou Cioffi, and Chris Schenkel. As they chatted, Roone spoke into Jim's earpiece with an update. Earlier reports had indicated that the hostages were OK. Now Jim had a few seconds to wrestle with how he would report the horrific news. He was hyper-aware that he was about to tell the Ohio parents of weight lifter David Berger, who was competing for Israel, that their son had been killed. Instead of using typical news lingo like "We now have final word," Jim found a way to set the tone and prepare the viewers, in particular the Berger family, for what he was about to tell them.

First, he addressed his colleagues. "When I was a kid, my father used to say, 'Our greatest hopes and our worst fears are seldom realized.' Our worst fears have been realized tonight." Jim then turned and faced the camera next to me. After his sixteen-hour, on-air marathon, he was unshaven and looked exhausted, forlorn. His next words seemed very personal. I'm sure that every viewer at home felt as I did standing only a few feet from him in the studio: Jim was talking privately to each one of us. He was not a commentator, but a friend, putting his hand on your shoulder as he relayed a hard truth.

"There were eleven hostages. Two were killed in their rooms yesterday morning. Nine were killed at the airport tonight. They're all gone."

It was over. The news was numbing. There was nothing anyone could do. The Munich Games, along with the Olympic ideal, had been tarnished for all time. True, there had always been political controversies surrounding the Olympics, even during their ancient incarnations in Greece. As recently as 1968, thousands of students in Mexico City had protested the repressive government only ten days before the Mexico City Games began. They had been hoping to gain worldwide attention with all the media in town. That they did, especially because they were fired on by police and military forces, and over two hundred people died. Yes, the history of the Olympics was rife with scandal, politics, bribery, professionalism, and protests, but never had there been terrorism. Never had Olympians been murdered during an Olympic Games. The Olympic spirit had always risen above the fray, but the Munich Massacre seemed insurmountable. What would happen?

The Games were suspended for the first time in modern Olympic history. A memorial gathering was held in the stadium. Suddenly, "town meeting of the world" had a different import. Many people—including Willi Daume, president of the Munich Organizing Committee—wanted the games canceled. Emotional debate was heard everywhere. I remember a discussion while jogging along the Isar River with another colleague, Erich Segal, author of the best-selling *Love Story*. Roone had hired Erich as an expert commentator for the marathon because he was also a long-distance runner. Erich felt that the Games should be ended in honor of the dead Israelis. I wanted to honor the dead Israelis, but I also wanted the Games to continue.

At the memorial service, Brundage declared that "The Games must go on." He was applauded in the stadium when he said this, but he was also widely criticized. Personally, I agreed with Brundage. If the Games did not resume, then the terrorists would have prevailed over the Olympic spirit.

The surviving Israeli athletes went home. Mark Spitz, the American swimming sensation, who won an unprecedented seven gold medals and set seven world records during the first week of competition, had already left West Germany under heavy guard. Some feared he might be another target because he was Jewish. Some athletes left the Games on their own. The party was over for them. The Olympic Movement, chartered to build peace and a better world by educating youth through sport, now had murder in its DNA, and a well-intentioned host city became forever branded as the birthplace of modern Islamic terrorism.

When competition resumed, it was tough to carry on. The tragedy overshadowed every story, every competition, which is probably why I remember so little about the second week. On the final day of the Games, Jim and I took a walk together beneath the Olympic Stadium grandstands in the early morning. He thought aloud about how to handle his hosting duties that evening during the Closing Ceremony. I thought about our visit to the stadium earlier in the year, when it was still under construction. At the time, things were in a state of disarray, but the oval track was in place. We took a lap and jogged along, leaping over occasional piles of building materials as if they were obstacles in a steeplechase, then "raced" toward the finish, crossing it shoulder to shoulder while raising our arms as we broke an imaginary tape. We even took silly pride in knowing that we two, albeit briefly, would hold the record for the fastest time on the Olympiastadion track. We also contemplated all the great moments that would take place there during the Games.

Now, in September, we were trying to find a way to eulogize the Israeli dead in the framework of the Olympic spirit. Jim said he recalled some poem about a young athlete dying. I told him I read that poem in my English poetry class in college, and the book was on a shelf in my living room. As it was decades before we could simply "Google it," I called Debbie, who retrieved the book and read A. E. Housman's poem to me while I wrote it down. Jim read most of the poem during the Closing Ceremony:

> The time you won your town the race
> We chaired you through the market-place;
> Man and boy stood cheering by,
> And home we brought you shoulder-high.
>
> To-day, the road all runners come,
> Shoulder-high we bring you home,
> And set you at your threshold down,
> Townsman of a stiller town.

Smart lad, to slip betimes away
From fields where glory does not stay,
And early though the laurel grows
It withers quicker than the rose.

Eyes the shady night has shut
Cannot see the record cut,
And silence sounds no worse than cheers
After earth has stopped the ears:

Now you will not swell the rout
Of lads that wore their honours out,
Runners whom renown outran
And the name died before the man.

So set, before its echoes fade,
The fleet foot on the sill of shade,
And hold to the low lintel up
The still-defended challenge-cup.

When we arrived at the Munich airport to go home, we were welcomed to a "new normal" by having to go through full security searches
for the first time. It was also the only time during my fifty years at ABC
that the network chartered a plane to fly us all back to the United States
nonstop. I'm not sure whether this was a security measure or just a way
to keep some of us together for the journey home. We were all in the
television sports production business, but we had just reported one of
the great news tragedies of the twentieth century. We were proud of the
job we had done, but there was an undercurrent of darkness among us.
Today, decades later, we've come to expect such news stories about jihad-
ist atrocities and people blowing themselves up in crowds of innocent
people as an act of martyrdom. But in Munich in 1972, we were shocked
by this kind of barbarity. The death of the Israeli athletes and such horror
at the Olympic Games were beyond comprehension. Prior to that atroc-
ity, for me, war and related violence had always occurred somewhere far

away—overseas in Europe or Korea or Vietnam. On that September day in Munich, we were in the middle of it, and we had the responsibility of reporting it.

As we flew home, we all knew our lives would never be the same. The Olympic Games wouldn't be, either. The casual town meeting atmosphere was gone forever. All future Olympic Games would be held under tight security, and Olympic Villages would be locked down. As Jim McKay said years later in an interview, "It was the end of innocence in sports."

11

Closing Ceremony

The years went by, and the times kept a-changin'. We began the year 1984 with the Sarajevo Winter Olympics, which featured marquee performances by Scott Hamilton, Katarina Witt, Torvill and Dean, downhill gold medalist Bill Johnson, and slalom stars Phil and Steve Mahre. The Triple Crown races, Indy 500, US Open, PGA, British Open, and NASCAR events also drew high ratings that year, but the culmination was our coverage of the Summer Games in Los Angeles. The wrap party in Los Angeles was beyond extravagance. We all felt like we were riding the crest of a wave of success that had been building since the early 1960s. Little did we know that the half-million-dollar celebration would turn out to be the last hurrah for ABC Sports.

The following year, Leonard Goldenson, the admirable and brilliant CEO who brought the third network from oblivion to equal footing with CBS and NBC, handed the management reins over to ABC's new owner, Capital Cities Communications. Capital Cities was a Wall Street favorite but, in comparison to ABC, a small company. Roone characterized the merger as "the canary swallowing the cat." Over the years, Goldenson had fought off unwelcome takeovers by the likes of Harold Geneen of ITT and Howard Hughes, but he had handpicked Thomas Murphy and Daniel Burke of Capital Cities to take the baton. Goldenson was a visionary and sensed that a new age in television was on the horizon. ABC had to keep evolving. The network had already added enough affiliates to be competitive with CBS and NBC, but cable television was starting to eat away at audience shares. ABC's prime-time entertainment ratings, which had finally surpassed the Big Two during the 1976–77 season, were in decline. Given his actions, I don't think Goldenson had full confidence that his immediate staff could lead the company into the future. The parties concluded the transaction quietly over a weekend. None of us on the twenty-eighth floor had a clue the following Monday morning what was taking place on the thirty-seventh. I was lunching with Peggy Fleming and Roz Sumners in Manhattan when Irwin Weiner, administrative chief of ABC Sports, walked into the restaurant, noticed me, and told us that we no longer worked for ABC.

The new emphasis on the bottom line went into effect quickly. Where the twentieth-anniversary special in 1981 was a lavish, sit-down gala held in the Grand Ballroom of the Waldorf Astoria Hotel, the post-merger twenty-fifth anniversary special took place in one of our studios with grandstand seating and potato chips and soft drinks for refreshments. But the belt-tightening meant more than first-class entertainment and travel perks going by the wayside. It also seemed gradually to affect our broadcast excellence and to change the way we approached our shows.

The days of conducting site surveys prior to every event were over. There was no more returning to New York and submitting a proposal to administration, which had always pushed pencils to pay for it all. Now we were told what the budget would be *before* we left for a survey. If we didn't have enough money for a crane camera, we did without. Soon after the year 2000, we went from sending a team of people to events to sending just a couple. We also began producing events without being on site. Upon receipt of the foreign feed via satellite in New York, we would edit the subpar footage, then record the announcers over it. Viewers were likely not aware that the announcers never saw the event. For many of the Grand Prix Series telecasts, for instance, Peter Carruthers was on site to do interviews, which aided the illusion, but Terry Gannon and the expert commentators never left the Unites States! Their commentary was recorded while they watched video replay on monitors in New Jersey studios.

We lost all control of the coverage of many events. The goal became merely to get the event on the air. Admittedly, a lot of money was saved, but the focus of our creative energies became divided. We were challenged, with increasing desperation and decreasing budgets, to maintain the level of production quality for which we had become known and respected. Production wasn't too happy servicing the green-eyeshade guys, but the result was extraordinary marketplace success. Nine years after Capital Cities took over, the stock was at $740 a share when it split ten for one, the second most expensive stock on the New York Stock Exchange, behind Berkshire Hathaway, Inc.

More changes came about as new blood entered our ranks in the late 1980s and 1990s. These young producers and directors took a different approach to the storytelling process. They prepared for events and planned scene sets in detail before leaving. They didn't want to wing it. Although this method reflected the new corporate policies, I felt this style stifled the creative process. Such premeditation made an event fit a preconceived vision of it. My contemporaries and I had always done our research prior to an event, but then we learned more on the scene and "felt" it. Out of that experience, we would formulate our story, which seemed to communicate better to the audience what it was like to actually be there. Production on the fly was certainly less comfortable, but when covering unfamiliar events like the Lumberjack World Championships in a place like Hayward, Wisconsin, or a surfing competition on the monstrous waves of Oahu's North Shore, exploring the environs and the atmosphere and meeting all the colorful characters was part of telling the story—often the best part.

Back in 1979, the Entertainment and Sports Programming Network (ESPN) debuted on cable. Within one year, the first channel devoted exclusively to sports had a full schedule of programming. The folks at ESPN understandably felt that being purely focused on sports around the clock, they could delve into subjects more deeply than we could in a one-and-a-half-hour weekly sports anthology. They considered ESPN to be a competitor of ABC, an infant David waiting to take on the Sports Goliath.

ABC bought 80 percent of ESPN in 1984, but there remained an underlying sense of competition. We at ABC Sports, "Recognized around the world as the leader in sports television" as was said at the end of our telecasts in those days, paid little attention to the feud. After all, we had twenty-three years of tradition and broadcast dominance, but apparently not much foresight. We just kept doing our shows and wallowing in what now can clearly be seen as fading glory.

The Mouse moved into the house in 1995 when the Walt Disney Company bought Capital Cities/ABC. What Disney primarily had its eye on in the purchase was the ESPN brand. ESPN was already a worldwide cablecaster that would expand Disney's global communications network. At the time, the broadcast rights to the Sydney Olympics were in play, and bidding for the upcoming Winter Games in Salt Lake City was not far off. But Disney, along with the other networks, got trumped by NBC in a preemptive strike. Less than two days after the Disney acquisition, Dick Ebersol, the head of NBC Sports (and one-time assistant to Roone Arledge), hopped aboard a corporate jet to meet with the International Olympic Committee's television rights negotiator. The NBC contingent put forth a huge bid for an unprecedented two-Games package for a total of $1.2 billion with the condition that the other networks be excluded from negotiations. If the IOC refused and opted for the usual bidding process, NBC would make an offer, but at a lower price. The result? Ebersol returned home with the Olympics broadcast rights locked up for NBC for years to come. Brilliant.

Before long, ESPN executives were put in charge of ABC Sports, and it became clear which entity would eventually dominate the sibling rivalry. There were also some legal barriers to overcome involving the crossing over of cable into broadcast airwaves, union issues being one of them (ESPN was a nonunion shop). To add to our woes, ABC Sports had been operating in the red since 1992 due to the money spent to keep the broadcast rights for *Monday Night Football*. The simplest way to put an end to the financial drag would be to eliminate the division altogether.

On August 28, 2006, ABC Sports produced its last program, the final game of the Little League World Series. Producer Dick Buffinton initially wanted the telecast to serve as a tribute to the history and tradition of ABC Sports, but ESPN squelched that idea. How strange that the final episode of *Wide World of Sports* had no historical clips except some of Little League Baseball throughout the years. Commentator Brent Musburger, who was told not to talk about *Wide World* during the telecast, managed to find a way. At the end of the show, Brent cleverly used

Little League Baseball as a metaphor for the 120 other sports covered during our thirty-seven years on the air. "Nothing," he said, "has done more for the Little League World Series than the cameras of *Wide World of Sports*." The video image then dissolved from Brent in the booth to a shot of the ABC Sports logo emblazoned on the side of a mobile van.

From that moment on, the logo was retired and the tag line became "You're watching ESPN on ABC." To the general viewing audience, not much was about to change except for more sports programming originating on cable; but to those of us who had been with ABC Sports since almost the beginning, that final telecast felt like a funeral.

My career was winding down, too, and I directed mostly figure skating during my last few years. My last assignment was the 2008 World Championships in Göteborg, Sweden. As we all know, ESPN thrived and now covers, analyzes, and editorializes the sports universe daily on several channels. One channel is completely dedicated to sports news and another to rebroadcasting "classic" games and programs, including an occasional episode of *Wide World of Sports*. Between ESPN and other sports outlets, just about every game, match, or event, no matter what the sport or location, can be watched live on your television set, computer, smart phone, or tablet. "The Fun and Games Department," as Cosell used to call the sports division, is open all hours—which is probably a welcome respite for many people, considering that world news is now on multiple channels 24/7 as well.

With so many viewing options, choice has been vastly expanded, but exposure has diminished. Cathy Rigby became widely popular in the 1970s because she was a pioneer in gymnastics, the first American to win a world medal in a sport that was new and different to most Americans. But more significantly, Cathy was in the spotlight during a time when there were only three networks to watch, so her audience was much greater. As she pointed out during her interview with Ernie Manouse on his PBS show, *InnerVIEWS,* in 2010, "Nowadays with so much access to so much television, it's a little bit diluted."

The viewers' experience has been diluted, too. Look at Olympics coverage. In 1960, CBS produced only thirteen hours of coverage from the Squaw Valley Winter Games (and paid $50,000 for the broadcast rights). In 2012, NBC Universal broadcast 5,535 hours of London

Olympics coverage on NBC, MSNBC, Bravo, CNBC, NBC Sports, and NBCOlympics.com (for $1.18 billion). Today's television shares (the percentage of television sets actually in use and tuned to a certain program) rarely reach the highs of yesteryear because everyone isn't watching the same thing anymore. Yes, TV's golden age of sports is long past, but in today's "global community," does the programming have equal impact? It seems that in the era of limited channels, our shared television experiences were more intimate, more intense. So much so that in 1972, an athlete who competed in an obscure sport and didn't even win an Olympic medal (Cathy Rigby) became a household name, as did a Soviet weight lifter, of all people (Vasily Alekseyev)...and forty years later, anyone who was alive and watching then can remember all the details! I don't think that broadcasts since the late 1980s have had the same lasting impressions.

TV certainly *looks* better today. The panoramic images of rolling greens at the Augusta National Golf Club during the Masters are so vivid you can count the individual blades of grass; and what a rush to have an aerial gyro-stabilized camera show you what it's like to be an NFL quarterback under a blitz attack. These high-definition details on giant flat screens are such a long way from the fuzzy black-and-white images scanned together from the weak broadcast signals of the 1960s.

Better, though?

With all due respect, even awe, for microscopic clarity and life-size pictures, remember that television is still a medium for telling stories. How many times have you flipped through hundreds of channels only to complain there's nothing on? The fundamentals haven't changed and never will. A good story with conflict and drama and intriguing characters, and told well, will lock in a viewer. That is precisely why *Wide World of Sports* was able to pull in so many people who weren't even sports fans. Have today's producers lost faith in this principle? There seems to be an undercurrent of frenzy flashing across the TV screen continuously. It's as though they are desperate not to let more than a few seconds pass without some energizing motion, some flash or flicker that will keep the viewer staring at the screen. The priority isn't storytelling anymore, it's attention holding. Style overrides content.

If you were alive and watching *Monday Night Football* during the 1970s, the first thing you remember isn't any of the players or the teams that won, or even innovative production techniques. It's the three men in the booth. And you can name each one of them: Howard Cosell, "Dandy Don" Meredith, and Frank Gifford. The main reason for *MNF*'s success was that it was entertaining! Even if the game was terrible, the three men in the yellow blazers gave everyone something to talk about at the water-cooler on Tuesday morning. These days, there's not only *Monday Night Football*, there's also *Sunday Night Football* and *Thursday Night Football*…

We've all been around the planet several times now, even if we've never left our couches or computer chairs. This reality has left a huge challenge for today's production crews, but I think that ABC Sports' wide-angle view was quite different than ESPN's more narrow focus. We talked about geography and world wars and Khrushchev and Kennedy, and we tried to put sporting events into the context of world events. NBC's Olympic telecasts have certainly strived for that bigger picture, which reminds me of a phone call Jim McKay told me he received from Bob Costas and Dick Ebersol during NBC's coverage of the 1992 Summer Olympics in Barcelona. They asked Jim how they were doing, and after Jim's complimentary reply, Ebersol remarked, "You made the blueprint. We're just trying to follow it."

Epilogue

"Champagne in paper cups."

Jim never forgot that phrase. He felt it was the perfect description of life on the ABC Sports treadmill. So true. Our globe-trotting jobs had us savoring pressed duck at the centuries-old La Tour d'Argent in Paris while looking out over the Seine and Notre Dame; sipping Stolichnaya and nibbling beluga caviar on a Swissair flight when such Russian delicacies weren't available in the States; and seemingly living the lifestyles of the rich and famous. Truth was we enjoyed all those perks, but fleetingly, because we usually worked around the clock. Even when I returned to New York, on many occasions I went directly from the airport to the tape room to edit, then slept on a bed of videotape boxes.

From the outside we were envied, and that envy was well placed. However, there were downsides, such as extraordinary stress, sleep deprivation, and absence from our families. My late wife, Debbie, said that she didn't mind it so much when I was on the road; but when I was home, I wasn't really home. On one occasion, I walked through the front door with my suitcase in hand and my nine-year-old son, Jamie, shouted, "Hey, Mom, we have a visitor!"

Roone deliberately hired people who were willing to make ABC Sports the center of their lives. I was one of them. I was on the road six to seven months a year for decades and rarely took a vacation. Even when

I slowed down enough to join a family dinner, I was still on the job, or rather, still talking about it. I wanted my wife and boys to hear all about Bratislava and Kitzbühel, Tokyo and London, Dorothy Hamill and Evel Knievel. I wanted to be the big hero—the guy jetting around the world to major sporting events, not the guy taking out the garbage! But it took me way too long to learn that my sons wanted to tell me about *their* lives and experiences and what was going on at school. They wanted a father, but I was terribly self-absorbed. I couldn't turn off the TV spotlight and fully become a spouse and father. To compound the situation, I was also constantly worrying about the next assignment because I was haunted by the fear of failure.

At the heart of it all, I was insensitive to the pressure on my wife raising three sons on her own. When she was pregnant with our third child in 1965, I was in Rome, working on the team that made television history by linking up a track meet in Kiev with the United States. When I got home, I was so exhausted, I crashed. The next day, Debbie and I were sitting in our living room. She was on the couch, and I was in an easy chair across from her.

"By the way," she said casually, "I had a miscarriage."

I was stunned. I felt terrible that I wasn't there for her.

"Why didn't you call me?"

"What good would that have done?" She explained that I couldn't have gotten home in time to help her through it, and my worrying would have only made it more difficult for me to do my job.

In 1988, Debbie accompanied me to the Calgary Olympics. I had huge responsibilities that year directing both figure skating and the Closing Ceremony. On the last Saturday, I had just finished the ladies' free skate telecast and rushed over for the dress rehearsal for the Closing Ceremony. It was a disaster. Every camera shot planned over months of preparation was off the mark. I got back to the hotel about 2:00 a.m. to find Debbie asleep. She didn't wake up, but just her presence settled me down and relieved my panic. I rested for a few hours, then returned to the production trailer to re-block the show. I learned then that home wasn't where my house was—it was where my wife was.

That summer, Debbie was diagnosed with esophageal cancer. Throughout her illness, I came to believe that the immune system is deeply affected by stress. I know I put Debbie through an inordinate amount of stress. She also smoked, not heavily, but always had a couple of cigarettes in the evening with a vodka and soda. The statistics are there in terms of what those cause. First, she lost half her larynx. Then the cancer appeared in her esophagus. She was given an option, which she accepted, to cut her open and pull up her stomach and attach it to the back of her throat. During the surgery, they found that the cancer had metastasized, so they stopped and sewed her back up.

Dennis Swanson, Roone's successor at ABC Sports, took me off a skating assignment in Moscow because he felt it put me too far away from Debbie. I told him that Debbie and I had talked it over and made a plan, so we were prepared. He wouldn't hear of it. Later, when the event in Moscow was in progress and Debbie was in dire straits, all I could think was thank God and Dennis Swanson that I wasn't in Moscow.

Debbie died in 1991. To this day, I still feel guilty about the career that took me away from my family and left Debbie as a single mom. I could not have done what she did, raising three boys mostly on her own. I also hope for our sons, Ted, Jamie, and Peter, that growing up with a father who was usually in another time zone wasn't too detrimental. Apparently, my career had some appeal, though, as two of them went into the television business, one in news and the other in cable management.

I loved my job. Really loved it. But it was like an addiction. Total physical and emotional immersion. Euphoric highs and anxious lows. The thrill of victory and the agony of defeat. Nevertheless, with the exception of being more present for my family, I'd do it all again.

"The Wide World"

Written by Doug Wilson and performed on
ABC's Wide World of Sports' Tenth Anniversary Special in 1971

Years ago I boarded a plane to
search in the world of sport
To see how we live side by side in conflict of every sort
I traveled to the playing fields of
England's sporting clime
And watched them in an Irish hurling battle

> Over the wide, wide world
> Over the wide, wide world
> There is a plan
> We can shake hands and understand

I passed through time zones endlessly
to see them east and west
Do their thing incessantly trying to be the best

I've seen the slashing competitive
clashing in sport of every kind
And when it's done they touch and walk together

> (Chorus)

I've watched them challenge mountainsides
to get there before another
At times in teams go head-to-head
victoriously crushing the other
I watched them try to reach beyond
the boundaries of speed
And overcome their inborn limitations

> (Chorus)

The world of sport is everyone who
acts in human fashion
Racing after what we want, committed to our passion
We have seen in other worlds this sporting way prevail
So when it's done, we all will walk together

> Over the wide, wide world
> Over our wonderful wide world
> Yes, there is a plan
> That can bring peace to every land

Credit Roll

George C. Scott said that director Mike Nichols created an atmosphere in which "you [were] free to experiment and explore." I felt such freedom working under Roone Arledge, Chuck Howard, Jim Spence, Dennis Swanson, Dennis Lewin, Geoffrey Mason, Bob Apter, Howard Katz, and Mike Pearl. More importantly, I was the beneficiary of the outstanding work of an untold number of people. I'm eager to acknowledge them.

To Mac Hemion, for whom I did those cue cards on my first day at ABC in 1958. He used to say that a director is only as good as his cameramen. Whatever success I had in my work as a director, especially in figure skating, I owe to hundreds of camera people, among them: Dianne Cates, Tom O'Connell, John Brunn, Scott Staton, Ed Martino, Mike Freedman, Bill Sullivan, John Morealle, John "Peaches" Langford, Evan Baker, Dale Walsh, Sal Folino, Larry Neucam, Larry Stenman, D. J. Diomedes, George Montanez, Drew DeRosa, John Duncum, Harry Hart, Kirk Hepburn, Frank Melchiore, Andrew Lottridge, Alf Carboni, Graham Maunder, Jack Cronin, Jack Schaefer, Don Shoemaker, Steve Nikafor, and Warren Cress.

I'd like to express my admiration and respect for so many fellow associate directors, directors, and producers who brought *Wide World* to life every week, among them: Marvin Schlenker, Ronnie Hawkins, Dick Kirchner, Bill Bennington, Jim Holmes, Larry Kamm, Bob Goodrich,

Jim Jennett, Lou Frederick, Eleanor Riger, Carol Lehti, Vince DeDario, Brice Weisman, Amy Sacks, Emilie Deutsch, Joe Bush, David Kiviat, Toni Slotkin, Terry Jastrow, Ed Nadel, Don Ohlmeyer, and of course, Chet Forte.

I'd also like to thank some amazing technical directors: John Broderick, Bill Morris, "Wink" Gunther, Walk Kubilus, Bob Bernthal, Gary Larkins, John "Zip" Zipay, and especially Joe Schiavo, who knew what I meant, despite what I said over the headset; and the audio engineers, who captured the indispensable sounds at events: Dick Roes, Jack Hughes, Jim Davis, Don Scholtis, Pete Addams, and Jack Kestenbaum, among many others. And to the king of supervising engineers, Stu Strelzer, who possessed an unwavering respect for the crew, an understanding of each production's goal, and the know-how to fix any technical problem.

A tip of my hat to the videotape editors, especially during the early years when they did their work with microscopes and razor blades. This incredible group of very patient professionals met deadline after deadline, working extremely long hours: Alex Moskovic, Pam Peterson, Mike Winnick, Bruce Giarraffa, Connie Kraus, Lou Rende, Mario Schencman, Victor Gonzalez, Bob Hersh, Lou Torino, Leo Stephan, Joe Longo, Marvin Gench, George Boetcher, and Jerry Cavajohn (who once fell asleep while standing with his eye resting on the microscope eyepiece!). I'm especially grateful to Scott Lozea, videotape editor extraordinaire, who has been making me look good for more years than I would like to admit, not only at ABC but also with my one-man shows.

To the unsung heroes who guided us in foreign lands: Jacques Lesgards, Georges Croses, Ray Falk, Chris Evans, and Kurt Fuchs. They garnered rights, supervised engineering, obtained facilities, and coordinated our comings and goings.

The cast of on-camera talent at ABC was a producer's dream, perhaps because so many of our early commentators, like McKay, hailed from a journalism background. They weaved our crews' pictures and sounds together with their creatively descriptive words. Men like Jack Whitaker, who was often charged with summarizing an event at its conclusion. He felt the heartbeat of every event he covered and was exceptional in his ability to communicate to the viewers at home. It was an honor to have worked with him, as well as so many others: Al Michaels, Bill Flemming, Chris Schenkel, Keith Jackson, Vern Lundquist, Al Trautwig, Bud Palmer, Dave Diles, Curt Gowdy, Howard Cosell, and Frank Gifford (whom I also thank for that time he got me out of harm's way underneath the whirling blades of a helicopter!). Special thanks to Terry Gannon, the consummate professional, who began hosting our skating telecasts in the 1990s, and who customarily got it right on take one.

And to our expert commentators, who became legends beyond their athletic accomplishments: Olympic swimmer Donna de Varona, who helped lead the fight for Title IX and was the first president of the Women's Sports Foundation; ski coach Bob Beattie, who was a key figure in the creation of the World Cup ski circuit and subsequently formed World Pro Skiing where skiers raced side by side; gymnasts Bart Conner and Nadia Comaneci, who oversee the International Gymnastics Hall of Fame; and Pittsburgh Steelers' wide receiver Lynn Swann (known to Cresta riders as The Flying Swan), who ventured into politics and served as the Chairman of the President's Council on Physical Fitness. And others, including Jackie Stewart, Sam Posey, Gordon Maddux, Kathy Johnson, Susie Wynn, Peter Carruthers, Kurt Browning, Paul Wylie, Arthur Ashe, Cliff Drysdale, Leo Durocher, Bruce Jenner, Eddie Arcaro, Paul Christman, Lee Grosscup, and Willie Mosconi, all of whom remain icons in their respective sports. And finally, Peggy Fleming, a national treasure, to whom I am also deeply indebted for her touching foreword. What an honor to have worked with all of these people.

As my forty-five years working in the sport of figure skating are near and dear to me, I must thank producer Dennis Lewin, who revitalized my directing career when it was on thin ice in 1981. And thanks to Joel Feld, the producer of skating events in the early 1990s, who always made me feel strong in the chair next to him. He was especially sensitive when Debbie was sick, while at the same time making me feel indispensable to the productions. I must also express my gratitude to Michelle Kwan, who was always welcoming and accessible to our ABC crews. How this gracious and beloved champion conducted herself in both victory and defeat kept interest in figure skating at a high level during the decade in which she dominated the sport. And finally, Dick Button, the expert commentator who can claim the longest run with ABC Sports. He began enlightening the American public about figure skating way back in the 1960s. More than anyone, Dick taught me how to appreciate skating artistry and guided me in how it should be seen.

I am proud to have started my career with Curt Gowdy Sr. and to have ended it with his son, Curt Gowdy Jr., who produced most of the skating telecasts after Disney took over. He's the man who had to deal with great changes in the company, while leading us all in our efforts to maintain levels of excellence despite being limited by budgetary constraints. Thanks to David Winner, who then took over the producing reins in 2007. David reminded us all in our first production meeting how lucky we were to be doing what we were doing and to work as a team and take chances—this was a wonderful environment in which to work during my last two years at ABC.

My thanks to Gary Smith and the late Dwight Hemion for the graduate course they gave me in variety television. Working with the Babe Ruths of prime-time entertainment, even for a brief time, was a dream come true for this sandlot kid.

I was sixty when Disney took over ABC in 1995, and one of the last things Dennis Swanson did as president of ABC Sports was to secure an unprecedented five-year contract that guaranteed my employment until age sixty-five. When new management took over, executive producer Pat Lowry was put in charge of figure skating for ESPN. She was particularly tuned into my work, being a director herself. With the support of Mike Pearl, then the division executive producer, and Bob Apter, vice president of administration, Pat saw to it that my career extended another eight years. Without Pat's and Dennis's foresight, it's unlikely I could have written this book from the vantage point of fifty years.

I raise my glass to Meg Streeter-Lauck and Tami Mickle, who, between them, worked at my side for twenty-six years. I'm eternally grateful for their patience and steadfast devotion as my assistants from just prior to the Sarajevo Olympics in 1984 through the World Championships in Göteborg in 2008. My gratitude goes also to former Canadian champion Lynn Nightingale, former US ice dance champion Judy Blumberg, Lana Sherman, Yvonne Gomez, and Jeff Cohan, who substituted for Meg and Tami on occasion. Also thanks to Jeff Nolt, who took over for Meg and introduced Tami to the camera blocking process. And kudos to Harriet

Hochberg, our skating production manager, who took care of all of us on the skating crew as a mama lion would her cubs.

My colleagues at ABC were like family, especially when Debbie took a turn for the worse. There were two people who gave me invaluable support during that trying time. One was Alex Wallau, then our boxing analyst and a cancer survivor himself, who helped educate me about the disease; the other was Diana Nyad, the indomitable long-distance swimmer, whose coaching prior to Debbie's memorial service was a godsend.

Much gratitude to flugelhorn player and composer Chuck Mangione, who made his music available for the soundtrack of our Lake Placid Olympic special and wrote the theme music for our 1980 Olympic telecast. I also referred to him as my psychiatrist because his music calmed me during my drive into work. Thank you, Maestro, for also playing at Betsy's and my wedding. "Feel So Good" never felt better.

One of the ancillary joys of writing this book was making phone calls to friends and associates to make sure I was "telling it like it was." My deepest thanks to Geoffrey Mason for our many discussions about the details of the Munich tragedy; and to Dick Buffinton, Jim Jennett, and Dennis Lewin, on whom I imposed many times to recall details. I also enjoyed chatting with Elaine Zayak, Janet Lynn, Sara Hughes, Jim Spence, Roger Goodman, Jack Gallivan, Jack Fitzgerald, Dennis Swanson, Bob Apter, Mike Pearl, Carol Lehti, Jamie Bravo, Bob Goodrich, Bob Lanning, Trixi Schuba, Dick Button, Norm Samet, Jirina Ribbens, Dick Ellis, Patty Rodiloso Wolfe, Lydia Stephans, Bob Beattie, Phyllis Howard, David Raith, Marilyn Kammer, Louise Argianis, Ann Marie DeBlasio, Gary Smith, Don Mischer, John Wilcox, and Ralph Mellanby. Everyone seemed to share the excitement of those ABC Sports years and these delightful conversations widened the curtain of my memory.

I am also indebted to Ralph Mellanby, the Roone Arledge of Canadian television and the executive producer of the host broadcast of the Calgary Olympics in 1988. By talking Roone into loaning me to him for the Games to direct the worldwide figure skating feed as well as the Closing Ceremony, Ralph raised the level of respect I had in my career. I am also grateful to William Taaffe of *Sports Illustrated* for the feature he wrote just prior to the Calgary Games, which dramatically expanded awareness of my work.

I present a shiny, red apple to Miss Daley, my sixth-grade teacher, who taught me and the other boys in my class to respect the "gentler sex." She always played on the girls' teams against us boys, and after getting beaten by them in dodgeball, soccer, and softball, we boys learned that women are strong, both physically and mentally. Miss Daley's advice surely came in handy when women joined the ABC team during the second decade of my career.

My pen genuflects to the members of my writers group: Stan Fried, Ed Blair, Emma Lou Sailors, Ed Drake, Tom Brennan, Jeanne Zaino, and to our leader, Carol Barkin, who has guided my literary journey over many years.

Jody and I are very appreciative to the readers who critiqued our efforts at various stages of the writing process: Betsy Griggs Wilson (my numero uno), Karen French, Christine Brennan, Kate Buford, Barrett Seaman, David Raith, Anthony Kazmierczak, Susan Russell, Amy Sherwood, Charmian Cohen, Rochelle Lindsey, Todd Davidson, Buz Cohan, Mike Kichaven, Mike Davis, Carol Davis, and Stacey Powells-Lyster (who also did our music clearance and permissions). Thanks also to Elizabeth Trupin-Pulli, Richard Greenstone, Marc Martino, BJ Robbins, Phil Maley, and Meg Ruley for their expert advice along the way.

A toast to Ann Limongello and Ida Astute, who patiently led me through the ABC photo archives; and to Kim Dejno, who found precious shots that have also been included. Thanks to Marilyn Kammer and Louise Argianis, ABC colleagues for many years, who were essential in accomplishing some of our video research. And thanks to Kristy Schmitt and Linda Merlos of Irvington Printing, and Stephen Ingle, Joanne Anderson, and Barbara Holloway of WordCo Indexing Services.

We applaud our production team at CreateSpace: Ashley Strosnider, Danna Mathias, Kerrie Robertson, and Chris Willemse; and we bow to Joseph Sigalas, Susan W. Sigalas, Tara Horton, and Barbara Schuetz for their insightful and thorough editing. We also thank Chinh Ngo and Aleen Johnson Ferris for their help with the segment graphics.

Christine Brennan, Dick Button, Nadia Comaneci, Bart Conner, Curt Gowdy Jr., Scott Hamilton, Jim Jennett, Carley Johnson, Billie Jean King, Sean McManus, Al Michaels, Barrett Seaman, and Lesley Visser, thank you for such enthusiastic support. We are honored. We also greatly appreciate the efforts of everyone at United States Figure Skating and its executive director David Raith. They were instrumental in getting the word out about this book.

The influence of Betsy Parker Thorndike Griggs Wilson, my very patient spouse, is imbued in every line of this book. For years, she has lived with its evolution. Without her encouragement and acumen, this book would never have happened.

How does a father thank his sons? They had to handle things alone... a lot. They did it. They were great sons to their mother and have been wonderful in my second life with Betsy. I hope they know how very proud I am of each of them. And to my older brother, John, who has looked out for me since infancy. It is impossible to document the scope of his support and advice, and to characterize the depth of inspiration he has provided. He's always been there...for the book, for my shows, for life. And to my late brother, David, who was a brilliant columnist for the *Boston Globe.* He was my literary idol. When Lesley Visser read the book and told me that David would have been proud, she gifted me the ultimate tribute.

To the late Linda Marmelstein, with whom I worked on an Arthur Godfrey special about the Calgary Stampede in 1969. Throughout the decades, her first words to me on the phone were always, "How's the book coming?" I was later encouraged to write a book by D. T. Slouffman. When he joined our ABC team as a young man, he told me that younger generations would be eager to read about early television. And to any of my colleagues whom I forgot to mention as this credit roll comes to an end, please forgive me.

As my career at ABC began to ebb, I finally got serious about recording my travels and experiences for my sons—and their sons and daughters. But I wasn't a pro. I lacked the discipline and focus required to write a book. I needed help. Through my friend, figure-skating champion Tim Wood, I met Jody Cohan. I learned right away that she was an athlete and, while growing up, had been a devoted fan of ABC Sports, in particular *ABC's Wide World of Sports*, seldom missing a telecast. She knew, from a viewer's perspective, all the people, places, and events we had covered. More important, she understood the spirit with which many of us at ABC Sports approached our work. She "got it." She also grasped that our way of reporting sports wasn't just about performances, results, and statistics but was, as Peter Jennings put it, "about culture and nationalism and poli-tics, as well as individual human endeavor." The result of my collabora-tion with Jody is this book about my adventures, much more smoothly written than if I had done it alone, and enhanced by a professional who was able to appreciate deeply my sports odyssey and an extraordinary time in television and world history.

And, finally, to those who helped start my career: Mr. B., who intro-duced me to Mr. Como; and Harold Day, the fellow Colgate alum and vice president at ABC in 1958, who sent me to Bill Seamon, head of the Programming Department. Thank you, Bill, for hiring me. And a nod to Wiley Hance, the producer of public affairs programming for ABC in the late 1950s and '60s. In 1961, Wiley gave me my first opportunity to direct a television show. It was chancy. Thanks, Wiley. The gift lasted for half a century.

Index

Note: italic page numbers indicate photographs.

A

ABC, 2, *102*
    author's contract with, 1–2
    author's production assistant job at, 6
    and "Canvas of Ice" special, 107
    and ESPN, 153–154
    Dorothy Hamill's first special for, 58
    and Evel Knievel, 30
    maiden Olympic telecast of, 65
    merger with Capital Cities Communications, 151–153
    and Munich Massacre, 144, 149
    opening for, 9
    and payment for interviews, 36
    skating coverage for, 44–46
    sports programming of, 2–4
    women in workforce at, 136
    and World Figure Skating Championships, 119, 120
    and World Gold Skate Classic, 118, 119
ABC Music Library, 66–67
ABC News, 11, 14, 15, 139–140
ABC-Paramount Television, 3
ABC Sports, Inc., 3, *95,* 151–154
    Arledge as president of, 14
    and Munich Massacre, 8, 144–145
    and new NASCAR speedway, 76
    production perspective of, 157
    rights to Comaneci's final performance, 37

    women in workforce at, 130
    working conditions at, 159
ABC's Wide World of Sports, xiii
    1962 new opening for, 9
    approach to sports on, 7–8, 13, 157
    beginnings of, 1–4
    final episode of, 154–155
    "firsts" on, 7
    key team members of, 10
    quality of programs on, 156, 157
Aceti, Joe, 52–53
Addams, Pete, 166
AIDS, 124–126
Alabama International Motor Speedway, 76
Alekseyev, Vasily, 156
Ali, Muhammad, 21–26, 30, 67–68, *87, 88*
Ali, Rahman, 25
Allen, Scott, 127
American Broadcasting Company. *see* ABC
American culture
    expansion of consciousness in, 8–9
    shift in, 2
    and Vietnam War, 22
Anderson, Joanne, 170
Anton, Susan, 83
Apter, Bob, 165, 168, 169
Arcaro, Eddie, 167
Argianis, Louise, 169, 170
Aristotle, 146
Arledge, Roone Pinckney Jr., 3, 10–15,

86, 154, 165, 169

on ABC/Capital Cities merger, 151

Emmys of, 137

and Peggy Fleming, 45, 49

and Munich Massacre, 143–145

and Secretariat telecast, 79–80

vision of, xiii–xiv

Wilson hired by, 4

and Wilson's directorial debut, 42–43

and working conditions at ABC Sports, 159

and World Gold Skate Classic, 118–119

Arnaud, Leo, 65

Ashe, Arthur, *91,* 123–126, 167

Ashe, Camera, 125

Astute, Ida, 170

B

Bachial, Mr. (Mr. B.), 5, 172

Bader, Marvin, 112–114, 144

Baker, Evan, 165

Bardot, Brigitte, 114

Barkin, Carol, 170

baseball, Little League World Series, 154–155

BBC, 28

Beattie, Bob, 167, 169

Beaty, Jim, 4

Belousova, Lyudmila, 80–81, *93*

Belton, Kim, 39

Bennington, Bill, 165

Berezhnaya, Yelena, 128

Berger, David, 146

Berkshire Hathaway, Inc., 153

Bernthal, Bob, 166

Bezic, Sandra, 108–109

Big Ten Conference (1969,1970), 74

billiards, The Hustler's Tournament (1965), 66–67

Black September, 144

Blair, Ed, 170

Blumberg, Judy, 168

Bobick, Duane, 143, 144

bobsled racing, 111

Boetcher, George, 166

Bogataj, Vinko, *89, 90*

Boitano, Brian, *99*

Alaskan wilderness skating special, 45, 107–109

costarring with Witt, 62–63, 132, 133

women's comments about, 135

Boone, Pat, 6

boxing

1960 heavyweight championship fight, 103–104

1966 heavyweight championship fight, 67–68

1972 Olympics, 143, 144

1973 Monaco match, 12–13

Muhammad Ali, 21–26

Brandt, Willy, 145

Bravo, 156

Bravo, Jamie, 169

Brawn, Vicki, 14

Brennan, Christine, 170

Brennan, Tom, 170

British Open, 151

Broderick, John, 166

Browning, Kurt, 167

Brumel, Valery, 3–4

Brundage, Avery, 145, 147

Brunn, John, 165

Buffinton, Dick, 154, 169

Buford, Kate, 170

Burke, Daniel, 151

Burns, Robert, 49

Burrows, Peter, 59–60

Bush, Joe, 166

Button, Dick, 167–170

    and Challenge of the Champions, 119, 120

    disagreement with Jim McKay, 57

    on Peggy Fleming, 45

    on Dorothy Hamill, 55, 57

    on Scott Hamilton, 83

    on Trixi Schuba, 50, 53

C

Cagney, James, 32

Calgary Stampede (1971 and 1972), 17

camaraderie among athletes, 117

Candid Productions, 119, 121

"Canvas of Ice" special, 107–109

Capital Cities Communications, 151, 153, 154

Carboni, Alf, 165

Carruthers, Peter, 152, 167

Castro, Fidel, 2

Cates, Dianne, 165

Cavajohn, Jerry, 166

CBS, 2

    Perry Como on, 4

    and Disneyland, 3

    McKay's work at, 15

    and Munich Massacre, 144

    Olympic coverage by, 155

    sports programming of, 3

CBS News and Sports, 18

CBS Sports, *94*

Ceauşescu, Nicolae, 33, 37

Challenge of the Champions (1988), 119, 121

Chamberlain, Neville, 139

Champions All meet (gymnastics), 36

The Chesterfield Supper Club, 5–6

Chou Chia-sheng, 70–71

Christman, Paul, 167

Cioffi, Lou, 146

civil rights, 23

Clark, Dick, 6–7

Clay, Cassius Marcellus, 21. *see also* Ali, Muhammad

CNBC, 156

Cohan, Buz, 170

Cohan, Jeff, 168

Cohan, Jody, 171–172

Cohen, Charmian, 170

Cold War, 3–4, 119–123

Colgate University, 5, 6

Columbia Broadcasting System. *see* CBS

Columbia College, 11

Columbia University, scholarship ceremony at, 11–12

Comaneci, Nadia, 33–41, *89, 98,* 167, 170

Como, Perry, 4–6, 172

Conner, Bart, 41, 167, 170

Cook, Kathy, 132, 136

Cosell, Howard, 73–74, *87,* 167

    and Muhammad Ali, 22–24

    controversial behavior of, 106–107

    grammar of, 78–79

    and *Monday Night Football,* 157

    on sports division, 155

Costas, Bob, 157

Cress, Warren, 165

the Cresta Run, 110–116

Cronin, Jack, 165

Croses, Georges, 166

D

Daladier, Edouard, 139

Daley, Miss (teacher), 170

Daly, John, 27

Danzer, Emmerich, 127

Daume, Willi, 147

Davidson, Todd, 170

Davis, Betty, 63

Davis, Carol, 170

Davis, Jim, 166

Davis, Mike, 170

Day, Harold, 172

Days of Grace (Arthur Ashe), 125–126

Dean, Christopher, 45, 81, 151

DeBlasio, Ann Marie, 169

DeDario, Vince, 166

DeLeeuw, Dianne, 58

Denjno, Kim, 170

DeRosa, Drew, 165

Deutsch, Emilie, 166

de Varona, Donna, 167

The Dick Clark Show, 6

Diles, Dave, 167

Diomedes, D.J., 165

directing telecasts, 42–44

Disney, Roy, 3

Disney, Walt, 3

Dowd, Ned, 48

Drake, Ed, 170

Drysdale, Cliff, 167

Duncum, John, 165

Dunphy, Don, 21

Durocher, Leo, 167

Dylan, Bob, 2

E

Ebersol, Dick, 154, 157

Ellis, Dick, 169

Entertainment and Sports Programming Network (ESPN), 12, 153–155, 157

Evans, Chris, 166

Evel Knievel on Tour (Sheldon Saltman), 21

extreme sports, Evel Knievel, 26–32

F

Falk, Ray, 166

Fassi, Carlo, 57

Feld, Amy Sacks, 135

Feld, Joel, 167

Ferdinand (archduke of Austria), 16

Ferris, Aleen Johnson, 170

figure skating

    Brian Boitano, 107–109

    decline in popularity of, 128

    filming, 42–44

    Peggy Fleming, 45–49

    Dorothy Hamill, 55–59

    Scott Hamilton, 83–84

    Janet Lynn, 51–55

    Protopopov and Belousova, 80–81

    Irina Rodnina, 119–123

    Trixi Schuba, 50–55

    scoring scandals in, 126–129

    Rosalynn Sumners, 60–62

    Katarina Witt, 62–64

    Elaine Zayak, 59–60

see also World Figure Skating Championships

Firecracker 250 (1961), 76

Fitzgerald, Jack, 169

Fleming, Peggy, xiii–xv, 42, 45–49, *93, 101,* 152, 167

    1968 gold medal performance of, 129

    appeal of, 51

    on female skaters, 61

Flemming, Bill, 36, 71, 74, 167

Flynn, Errol, 114

Folino, Sal, 165

Folley, Zora, 23

football

    Big Ten Conference (1969,1970), 74

    Monday Night Football, 154, 156–157

Foreman, George, 30

Forte, Chet, 13, 67, 73, 133–134, 166

Fox, 12

France, Bill Jr., 76–77

France, Bill Sr., 76

Fraser, Ian, 58

Frazier, Joe, 21

Frederick, Lou, 166

Freedman, Mike, 165

French, Karen, 170

Fried, Stan, 170

Fuchs, Kurt, 166

G

Gallivan, Jack, 169

Games of the Olympiad. *see* Olympic Games

Gannon, Terry, 152, 167

Garden City Country Club, 4

Garlits, Don, 117

Gench, Marvin, 166

gender issues, 130–136

Geneen, Harold, 151

Genuine Risk, *94,* 130

Giarraffa, Bruce, 166

Gifford, Frank, 29–30, 157, 167

Gifford, Kathy Lee, 32

glasnost, 119

Godfrey, Arthur, 15

Goldenson, Leonard, 2–3, 151

golf, 151

Gomez, Yvonne, 168

Gonfrade, Lillian, 66–67

Gonzalez, Victor, 166

Goodman, Roger, 169

Goodrich, Bob, 165, 169

Gorbachev, Mikhail, 119

Gorshkov, Alexander, 52

Gowdy, Curt, 167

Gowdy, Curt, Jr., 168, 170

Gowdy, Curt, Sr., 4, 168

Grand Central Station (radio program), 44

Grans Prix, 152

Greenstone, Richard, 170

Greenstreet, Sydney, 16

Grigg, Debbie, 6. *see also* Wilson, Debbie Grigg

Grosscup, Lee, 167

Grossfeld, Muriel, 70

Guidry, Ron, 105

Gunther, "Wink," 166

gymnastics

    1972 Olympic Games, 140–143

    Nadia Comaneci, 33–41

USA/China meet (1973), 70–71

H

Hamill, Dorothy, 55–59, 77, *96, 98,* 129

Hamilton, Scott, 45, 83–84, *88,* 151, 170

Hance, Wiley, 172

Hart, Harry, 165

Hawkins, Ronnie, *88,* 165

Hayes, Woody, 74–75

Heiss, Carol, 51

Hemion, Dwight, 58, 77, 168

Hemion, Mac, 165

Hemmings, David, 27

Hepburn, Kirk, 165

Hersh, Bob, 166

Hibbitt, George W., 11

Hitler, Adolph, 138, 139

HIV/AIDS, 124–126

Hochberg, Harriet, 168–169

hockey, 1980 Olympic Games, 49

Holiday on Ice, 54

Holloway, Barbara, 170

Holmes, Jim, 165

Hongbo Zhao, 45

horse racing

Kentucky Derby, 82

training regimen, 76

Triple Crown, 79–80, 151

Horton, Tara, 170

Hour of Power, 32

Housman, A. E., 148–149

Howard, Chuck, 165

Howard, Phyllis, 169

Hughes, Howard, 151

Hughes, Jack, 166

Hughes, Sara, 169

Hunter, "Jungle Jim," 75, *92*

The Hustler's Tournament (1965), 66

I

ice dancing, Torvill and Dean, 81

ice skating. *see* figure skating

Indianapolis 500, 151

Ingle, Stephen, 170

International Olympic Committee (IOC), 145, 154

International Skating Union (ISU), 52, 59, 126, 128

International Special Olympics, 105–106

The International Toboggan Championship, 110

IOC (International Olympic Committee), 145, 154

Irving, Adele, 66–67

ISU. *see* International Skating Union

Ithaca College, 135

J

Jackson, Keith, 167

Jacques, Michael, 118

Jastrow, Terry, 166

Jenner, Bruce, 167

Jennett, Jim, 166, 169, 170

Jennings, Peter, 172

and Roone Arledge, 11, 15

and Munich Massacre, 145, 146

at Munich Olympics, 139–140

Johansson, Ingemar, 103–104

Johnson, Bill, 151

Johnson, Carley, 170

Johnson, Junior, 76

Johnson, Kathy, 167

Johnson, Magic, 125

K

Kamm, Larry, 165

Kammer, Marilyn, 169, 170

Karolyi, Bela, 34, 35, 37

Katz, Howard, 165

Kazmierczak, Anthony, 170

Kelly, Gene, 58

Kelly, Jack, 65

Kennedy, John F., 2, 105, 157

Kentucky Derby, 82, 130

Kestenbaum, Jack, 166

Khrushchev, Nikita, 2, 157

Kichaven, Mike, 170

King, Billie Jean, *97,* 130–132, 170

Kirchner, Dick, 165

Kiviat, David, 166

Klages, Bill, 58

Knievel, Robert Craig, Jr. (Evel Knievel), 24, 26–32, *87, 89, 101*

Koppel, Ted, 15

Korbut, Olga, *95,* 141–142

Kraus, Connie, 166

Kubilus, Walk, 166

Kwan, Michelle, *100,* 167

L

Lake Placid Olympic Center, 45

Langford, John "Peaches," 165

Lanning, Bob, 169

Larkins, Gary, 166

Lauberhorn downhill race (1972), 68–69, 75

Laurin, Lucien, 76, 79

Lehti, Carol, 69, 166, 169

Lesgards, Jacques, 166

Lewin, Dennis, 165, 167, 169

Limongello, Ann, 170

Lindsey, Rochelle, 170

Lipton Tennis Championships (1990), 123

Liston, Sonny, 21, 73

Little League World Series, 154–155

Login, Maria, 40

London, Brian, 67–68

Longhi, Stefano, 69

Longo, Joe, 166

Lorre, Peter, 16

Lottridge, Andrew, 165

Louis, Joe, 22

Lowry, Pat, 168

Lozea, Scott, 166

Ludwig I, king of Bavaria, 140

Lumberjack World Championships, 153

Lundquist, Vern, 167

Lynn, Janet, 51–55, 129, 169

M

Maccarthy, Fairchilds "Mac," 112, 115

Maddox, Lester, 23

Maddux, Donna, 142

Maddux, Gordon, 71, 141, 167

Madison Square Garden (MSG), 4, 70

Magnussen, Karen, 55

Mahre, Phil, 151

Mahre, Steve, 151

Maley, Phil, 170

Mangione, Chuck, *96,* 169

Manouse, Ernie, 155

Mao Tse-tung, 70

March, Darcy, 108–109

Marmelstein, Linda, 171

Marr, Bob, 25

Martino, Ed, 165

Martino, Marc, 170

Mason, Geoffrey, 143, 165, 169

Mathias, Danna, 170

Maunder, Graham, 165

McEnroe, John, 135

McKay, Jim, 4, 10, 15–19, *86, 94, 97*

    and Muhammad Ali, 25

    Arthur Ashe interviewed by, 125

    Nadia Comaneci interviewed by, 36

    and Howard Cosell's grammar, 78–79

    disagreement with Dick Button, 57

    on Peggy Fleming, 48

    on Olga Korbut, 141

    and Munich Massacre, 8, 143–146, 148, 150

    and music in televised sports, 66, 67, 69

    and NBC's Olympics coverage, 157

    on Olympic Games, 137

    and opening for *Wide World,* 9

    on Gerti Schanderl, 56

    and *Wide World of Sports* approach, 7

    and working conditions at ABC Sports, 159

McKay, Margaret, 16, 18

McManus, Sean, 18, *94,* 170

Melchiore, Frank, 165

Mellanby, Ralph, 169

Meredith, "Dandy Don," 157

Merlos, Linda, 170

Michaels, Al, 49, 106, 167, 170

Mickle, Tami, 168

Mischer, Don, 169

Monday Night Football, 154, 156–157

Montanez, George, 165

Morealle, John, 165

Morris, Bill, 166

Mosconi, Willie, 167

Moskovic, Alex, 166

Moss, Stirling, *97*

MSG (Madison Square Garden), 4, 70

MSNBC, 156

Muhammad, Jabir Herbert, 25

Muhammad, Wallace Fard, 25

Müller, Jutta, 62

Munich Agreement, 139

Munich Massacre, 8, 143–150

Munich Organizing Committee, 147

Murphy, Thomas, 151

Musburger, Brent, 154–155

music/sound, 65–67

    for 1966 heavyweight title fight, 67–68

    in figure skating, 109, 121–122

    for Lauberhorn downhill race, 68–69

    in telecasting, 65–67

    for USA/China gymnastics meet, 70–71

Mussolini, Benito, 139

My Gallant, 79

N

Nadel, Ed, 166

Nastase, Ilie "Nasty," 135

National Association for Stock Car Auto Racing (NASCAR), 76–77, 151

Nation of Islam, 25

NBC, 2
author's work at, 6
and Disneyland, 3
Olympics coverage by, 127,
154–157
NBC News, 11
NBCOlympics.com, 156
NBC Sports, 154–156
NBC Universal, 155–156
Neucam, Larry, 165
New York Athletic Club Indoor
Games, 4
NFL Films, 66
Ngo, Chinh, 170
Nichols, Mike, 165
Nightingale, Lynn, 168
Nightline, 15
Nikafor, Steve, 165
Nixon, Richard, 70, 130
Nolt, Jeff, 168
Noman, Eric van Haren, 68–69
Nyad, Diana, 169

O
O'Connell, Tom, 165
Ohio State University Buckeyes, 74–75
Ohlmeyer, Don, 144, 166
Olympic Games, 9
1936, 138
1968, 127
1972, 137–150
1976, 34, 58
1980, 45–49
1984, 40, 62, 81, 151
1988, 62–64, 107, 160
1998, 54–55
2002, 127–128

boycott of, 40
collaborators in coverage of, 10
Comaneci's 1976 performance, 34
credits soundtrack for telecasts, 69
fellowship among athletes in, 117
Munich hostage crisis, 8, 143–150
Rodnina's medals in, 119–120
skaters killed in plane crash, 45
television coverage of, 155–156
theme music for telecasts, 65
and title of "World's Greatest Athlete," 20
World War II suspension of, 143
Olympic Order, 37
Ormesher, Harry, 28

P
Pakhomova, Lyudmila, 52
Palmer, Bud, 167
Panait, Constantin, 33–34
Patterson, Floyd, 103–104
Paul, Bob, 46–47
Pearl, Mike, 165, 168, 169
Pelletier, David, 128
Penn Relays (1961), 3
Pera, Patrick, 127
Perry, Gaylord, 80
Peterson, Pam, 166
Petkevich, John Misha, 52
PGA, 151
Phelps, Michael, 20
Ping-Pong Diplomacy, 70
politics in sports, 117
Easter Bloc athletes during Cold
War, 119–123
figure skating scoring scandals,
126–129

gender issues, 130–136
    and HIV/AIDS, 124–126
    World Gold Skate Classic, 118–119
pool, The Hustler's Tournament
        (1965), 66–67
Posey, Sam, 110–111, 113, 167
Powells-Lyster, Stacey, 170
Prague Spring (1968), 122
Pratt, Bill, 77
Primetime Live, 15
Protopopov, Oleg, 80–81, *93*

Q
Quarry, Jerry, 23–24

R
Raith, David, 169–171
Rende, Lou, 166
Renick, Sam, 79
Rhines, David, 108
Rhode, Kimberly, 20
Ribbens, Jirina, 121, 169
Riefenstahl, Leni, 66
Rigby, Cathy, 34, 36, 140–141, 155, 156
Riger, Eleanor Sanger, 130, 166
Riggs, Bobby, *97,* 130–133
Riva Ridge, 76
Robbins, BJ, 170
Roberts, Fireball, 76
Robertson, Kerrie, 170
Robertson, Oscar, 130
Robinson, Jackie, 4
rodeo/national country fair
        Calgary Stampede (1971), 17
        Calgary Stampede (1972), 17
Rodnina, Irina, 52, 119–123
Roes, Dick, 166

roller skating, World Gold Skate Classic (1969), 118–119
Romanian Gymnastics Federation, 34–36, 40
Rudolph, Wilma, 3–4
Ruley, Meg, 170
Russell, Susan, 170

S
Sachs, Gunter, 114–115
Sacks, Amy, 166
Sailors, Emma Lou, 170
Salé, Jamie, 128
Saltman, Sheldon, 27
Samaranch, Juan Antonio, 37
Samet, Norm, 169
Sawyer, Diane, 15
Schaefer, Jack, 165
Schanderl, Gerti, 56–57
Schembechler, Bo, 74
Schencman, Mario, 166
Schenkel, Chris, 34, 39, 80, 146, 167
Scherick, Edgar J., 3
Schiavo, Joe, 166
Schlenker, Mavin, 165
Schmitt, Kristy, 170
Scholtis, Don, 166
Schranz, Karl, 75, *92*
Schuba, Beatrix "Trixi," 50–55, 169
Schuetz, Barbara, 170
Schuller, Robert, 32
Schwarz, Wolfgang, 127
scoring scandals, 126–129
Scott, George C., 165
Seamon, Barrett, 170
Seamon, Bill, 172
The Second Steak Theory, 12

Secretariat, 79–80

Segal, Erich, 147

Seydel, Frances Louise, 134

Sherman, Lana, 168

Sherwood, Amy, 170

Shoemaker, Don, 31–32, 165

Shriver, Eunice Kennedy, 104–106

Sigalas, Joseph, 170

Sigalas, Susan W., 170

Sikharulidze, Anton, 128

skiing, Lauberhorn downhill race
        (1972), 68–69, 75

Slotkin, Toni, 166

Slouffman, D. T., 171

Smirnova, Lyudmila, 120, 121

Smith, Gary, 58, 77, 168, 169

sound. see music/sound

sound bites, 73

from Lyudmila Belousova, 81

from Howard Cosell, 74

from Christopher Dean, 81

and Bill France, Jr., 77

from Scott Hamilton, 84

from Woody Hayes, 75

from Lucien Laurin, 76

from Sonny Liston, 73

from Jim McKay, 79

from Sam Renick, 80

from Karl Schranz, 75

from Bill Taaffe, 83

from Raquel Welch, 78

from Jack Whitaker, 82

Special Olympics, 105–106

Spence, Jim, 36, 110, 165, 169

Spitz, Mark, 147

Sports Illustrated "Kiss of Death,"
        82–83

Sports Programs, Inc., 3

Sports Spectacular (CBS), 3

St. Moritz Bobsleigh Club, 114

St. Moritz Tobogganing Club, 111

Staton, Scott, 165

Steinbrenner, George, 105

Stenman, Larry, 165

Stephan, Leo, 166

Stephans, Lydia, 169

Stevenson, Teófilo, 143, 144

Stewart, Jackie, 167

stock car racing, NASCAR, 76

Stokey, Mike, 103–104

Streeter-Lauck, Meg, 168

Strelzer, Stu, 166

Strosnider, Ashley, 170

Sullivan, Bill, 48, 93, 165

Sumners, Rosalynn, 60–62, 152

Swann, Lynn, 167

Swanson, Dennis, 161, 165, 168, 169

Sweat, Eddie, 80

T

Taaffe, William "Bill," 43, 82–83, 169

table tennis, World Table Tennis
        Championship (1973), 16–17

Talladega Superspeedway, 76

television

bringing view into movement, 48

changes in, 2

directing telecasts, 42–44

high-definition, 156

impact of sound/music in, 65–67

sports programs on, 3, 155–156

technology developments for, 129–130

tennis

Arthur Ashe, 123–126

"The Battle of the Sexes" (1973), 130–131

Lipton Tennis Championships (1990), 123

World Table Tennis Championship (1973), 16–17

terrorism

Munich Olympics crisis, 8, 143–150

post-World War II, 138

Theler, Cha Cha, 115–116

Thies, Nancy, 70–71

This Week with David Brinkley, 15

Thomas, Debi, 63–64

Thomas, Kurt, 34, 38–39

Thorpe, Jim, 20

Title IX, 130

tobogganing, the Cresta Run, 110–116

Toomey, Bill, 117

Torino, Lou, 166

Torvill, Jayne, 45, 81, 151

track and field, first televising of, 3

Trautwig, Al, 167

Triple Crown

1973, 79–80

1984, 151

Trupin-Pulli, Elizabeth, 170

Turcotte, Ron, 80

Turishcheva, Lyudmila, 141, 142

Tweedy, Penny Chenery, 79

20/20, 15

U

Ulanov, Alexei, 52, 120–122

United States Air Force Reserves, 6

United States Figure Skating, 171

University of Michigan, 134

University of Michigan Wolverines, 74

USA/China gymnastics meet (1973), 70–71

USA/USSR track and field meet (1961), 3–4

US Figure Skating Association, 45, 128

US Figure Skating Hall of Fame, 43

US National Figure Skating Championships, 42, 59–61, 127

US Olympic Hockey Team, 49

US Open (1968), 124, 151

V

Vietnam War, 22

Visconti, Gary, 127

Visser, Lesley, 170, 171

W

Wald, Richard "Dick," 11

Walde, Hans-Joachim, 117

Wallau, Alex, 169

Walsh, Dale, 165

Walt Disney Company, 3, 154, 168

Walters, Barbara, 11, 15

Weiner, Irwin, 152

Weisman, Brice, 166

Welch, Raquel, 77–78

Whitaker, Jack, 82, 115, 166–167

"The Wide World" (Doug Wilson), 163

Wilcox, John, 144, 169

Willemse, Chris, 170

Williams, Jimmy, 31–32

Williams, Joe, 129

Williams, Serena, 135

Williamson, C. K. (Keith), 113

Wilson, Betsy Parker Thorndike Griggs, 11, 169–171

Wilson, David, 4, 69, 171

Wilson, Debbie Grigg, 169
and author's travel, 7
death of, 125, 161
illness of, 123, 160–161
marriage to, 6
and Munich Massacre, 148
and Doug's working schedule, 159, 160
Wilson, Doug, 88, 89, 93, 94, 96, 99, 100
Wilson, Jamie, 159, 161, 171
Wilson, John, 171
Wilson, Peter, 161, 171
Wilson, Ted, 161, 171
Wimbledon, 124, 131
Winner, David, 168
Winnick, Mike, 166
Witt, Katarina, 62–64, 135, 151
Wolfe, Patty Rodiloso, 169
women
female athletes, 130–132
in the workplace, 132–136
women's movement, 131, 134
Women's Tennis Association, 131
Wood, Tim, 127, 129, 171
The World Cup of Gymnastics, 35–36
World Figure Skating Championships
1968, 127
1971, 50–54, 56
1972, 120
1973, 55, 120–121
1974, 56–57
1976, 58
1982, 59
2008, 155
ABC's lost rights to, 119
decline in popularity of, 128
tribute to deaths of 1961 US World

Team, 45
World Gold Skate Classic (1969), 118–119
World Gymnastics Championships (1979), 35
World News Tonight, 15
"The World's Greatest Athlete," 20
Muhammad Ali as, 21–26
Nadia Comaneci as, 33–41
Evel Knievel as, 26–32
World Table Tennis Championship (1973), 16–17
Wylie, Paul, 167
Wynn, Susie, 167

X
Xeu Shen, 45

Z
Zaino, Jeanne, 170
Zaitsev, Alexander, 120–121
Zayak, Elaine, 59–60, 169
"Zayak Rule," 59
Zipay, John "Zip," *100,* 166

About the Authors

DOUG WILSON

Doug Wilson started at ABC in 1958. Over the years, he spanned the globe with *ABC's Wide World of Sports,* producing and/or directing fifty-one different sports across five continents. He also participated in the production of ten Olympic Games telecasts and became recognized internationally as the premier director in figure skating.

Wilson won seventeen Emmys and was honored by the Directors Guild of America in 1994 with its Lifetime Achievement Award in Sports. In 1995, the United States Figure Skating Association presented Wilson with its Spirit of Giving Award, and he was inducted into the United States Figure Skating Hall of Fame in 2003. He was also the first recipient of The Frank Bare Award for service to gymnastics, presented by the International Gymnastics Hall of Fame.

Over the past decade, Wilson has performed "An Evening with Doug Wilson," a one-man show about his fifty-year odyssey with ABC Sports, at various venues around the country. He has also guest lectured at numerous colleges, including his alma mater, Colgate University. Wilson has three sons and three stepchildren, and lives in Irvington and Saugerties, New York, with his wife, Betsy. They have eight grandchildren.

JODY COHAN

Jody Cohan's book, *What If Your Prince Falls Off His Horse?—The Married Woman's Primer on Financial Planning,* won several awards, including top honors in the Business Category at the 2009 San Francisco Book Festival. From 2005 through 2010, Jody coauthored the *Procrastinator's SOS Planner.*

Jody holds a bachelor of arts in Motion Picture/Television from UCLA and also attended the American Film Institute as a Screenwriting Fellow. She has worked in film and television, teaches writing, and is a volunteer mentor for WriteGirl.

In her youth, Jody was a ski instructor and played tennis competitively. She later coached tennis at the high school level and also coordinated media center operations at three tournaments on the women's professional tennis tour from 1989 to 1993. Throughout her childhood, she spent Saturday afternoons sitting on the couch with her family watching *ABC's Wide World of Sports.*

Made in the USA
Charleston, SC
29 September 2013